THE LIBRARY
Wycliffe College Stonehouse
Gloucestershire, GL10 2JQ
Tel: 01453-820438

The Arab-Israeli conflict 1947-67

103684

Non-Fiction   956.04 BLE

Wycliffe College

Living Through History

THE ARAB-ISRAELI CONFLICT 1947-1967

HEATHER BLEANEY AND RICHARD LAWLESS

B.T. Batsford Ltd London

CONTENTS

THE ARAB-ISRAELI CONFLICT	3
ZIONISTS:	9
David Ben-Gurion	10
Menachem Begin	14
Moshe Dayan	18
ARABS:	23
Musa Alami	24
King Abdullah of Jordan	27
Gamal Abdul Nasser	31
OUTSIDERS:	36
Harry S. Truman	36
Count Folke Bernadotte	39
Sir Anthony Eden	43
THE UPROOTED:	47
Fawaz Turki	49
Yuval Aloni	51
Erika Lewin	54
Raymonda Hawa Tawil	56
GLOSSARY	60
DATE LIST	62
BOOKS FOR FURTHER READING	63
INDEX	64

Acknowledgments

The Authors and Publishers wish to thank the following for their kind permission to reproduce copyright illustrations: Arab Development Council, figures 15 and 17; Camera Press, figures 28, 35, 36 and 46; John Hillelson Agency Ltd, figure 23; The Hulton-Deutsch Collection, figures 6, 16, 26 and 31; Imapress, figure 38; Imperial War Museum, figure 43; Magnum Photos, figures 7, 9, 10, 12, 13, 14, 19, 20, 32, 34, 37, 39, 40, 41, 43, 45 and frontispiece; Popperfoto, figures 3, 4, 8, 11, 18, 21, 22, 25, 27, 29, 30 and 33.

The illustrations on the front cover: (top) Israeli troops arrive and conquer the Dome of the Rock in Jerusalem 1967 (Magnum Photos); (bottom left) two members of the Arab equivalent to a civilian defence force in their sandbagged position inside the Jaffa Gate, Jerusalem, 1948 (Popperfoto); (bottom right) Jews planting orange trees in the 1950s (Magnum Photos).

Frontispiece:
Palestinian refugees struggle across the blown-up Allenby bridge to Jordan's East Bank after the 1967 war.

© Heather Bleaney and Richard Lawless 1990
First published 1990

All rights reserved. No part of this publication may be reproduced, in any form or by any means, without permission from the Publisher

Typeset by Tek-Art Ltd, West Wickham, Kent
Printed and bound in Great Britain by
The Bath Press, Avon
for the publishers
B.T. Batsford Ltd
4 Fitzhardinge Street
London W1H 0AH

ISBN 0 7134 5990 5

THE ARAB-ISRAELI CONFLICT 1947-1967

The struggle between Israel and the Arabs is one of the most intractable of modern times. In essence, it is a struggle over land, and the seeds of conflict were sown by Britain during the First World War. Britain was fighting the Ottoman Empire, which was allied with Germany, and was anxious to preserve and extend British influence in the Middle East. In 1915, Britain agreed to recognize and support an independent Arab state in the area from present-day Saudi Arabia north to the present Turkish border if the Arabs would help them by rebelling against Turkish rule. Two years later, the British Foreign Secretary, Arthur Balfour, pledged British support for the establishment of a Jewish 'National Home' in Palestine, then a province of the Turkish Empire. In a letter sent to Lord Rothschild of the Zionist Federation, Balfour wrote:

His Majesty's Government view with favour the establishment in Palestine of a national home for the Jewish people, and will use their best endeavours to facilitate the achievement of this object, it being clearly understood that nothing shall be done which may prejudice the civil and religious rights of the existing non-Jewish communities in Palestine, or the rights and political status enjoyed by Jews in any other country.

The Ottoman Turks were defeated in 1918, and the victorious British and French divided up the Arab provinces of the Ottoman Empire between themselves. The Arab nationalists, who had hoped for independence on the strength of British promises, were disappointed. The newly-created League of Nations awarded France a Mandate over Syria and Lebanon and Britain one over Palestine and Iraq. The British eventually gave Iraq a measure of independence, but they immediately divided Palestine into two. They installed an Arab ruler in the new country of Transjordan and ruled the remainder of Palestine from London. The terms of the Mandate reaffirmed Britain's commitment to the building of a Jewish national home that had been enshrined in the Balfour Declaration. In the first few years, thousands of Jews came to live in Palestine, bringing the percentage of the population that was Jewish up from 8 per cent in 1918 to 11 per cent in 1922, but Jewish immigration then declined.

From the outset, the British administration was faced with the impossible task of trying to reconcile two opposing nationalist movements in Palestine. The Zionists wanted to build a Jewish state in Palestine, but the Arabs living there demanded their own independent Arab state and feared that the Zionists would take over their country. There were sporadic outbreaks of violence, and tensions began to rise.

In the 1930s, persecution of the Jews by the Nazi regime in Germany and Nazi-occupied Europe led to a dramatic increase in Jewish immigration to Palestine as Jews sought refuge there. Arab fears and protests intensified, and a full-scale rebellion broke out in 1936, which was not crushed until 1938. In 1939, the British government issued a White Paper outlining their future policy for Palestine. With war threatening in Europe, Britain did not wish to antagonize the Arabs further and to put vital strategic interests and Middle Eastern oil supplies at risk. The British intended to limit future Jewish immigration to Palestine and allow self-governing institutions which would be dominated by the Arab majority. For the Zionists in Palestine, the White Paper meant a betrayal of British promises at a time when the Jews in Europe were being deported to concentration camps and murdered.

After the Second World War, the Jews in Palestine, who had fought with the Allies, started to attack British personnel and installations in order to force the British out. Britain was exhausted by the war with Germany and had no stomach for an expensive and "squalid war" as Winston Churchill described it. On 18 February 1947, the British Foreign Secretary, Ernest Bevin, announced to the House of Commons that Britain had found that

> the Mandate has proved to be unworkable in practice, that the obligations undertaken to the two communities have been shown to be irreconcilable.

On 2 April 1947, Britain referred the Mandate back to the United Nations (UN), the successor to the League of Nations.

In November 1947, the UN approved a plan for the partition of Palestine into two parts: an Arab State and a Jewish State. Jerusalem was to be under a special international regime because of its religious significance to Christians, Jews and Muslims alike. The plan allotted 57 per cent of the area to the Jews, who at that time made up only about 30 per cent of the population and owned only 6 per cent of the land. The Arabs, who formed the large majority of the people, could not accept that most of their country should be given away. Even in the proposed Jewish State there would be more Arabs than Jews. The Arabs rejected the plan out of hand. The Jews decided to accept partition, since it would give them at least a small Jewish state, though the Zionists never intended to content themselves with the boundaries proposed by the UN plan.

When the Partition plan was approved, violence broke out between Arabs and Jews in Palestine, and some 1700 people were killed. Alarmed, the UN began to reconsider the plan. Britain announced that it would leave Palestine on 15 May 1948. The Jewish Agency feared that victory would be snatched away from them at the eleventh hour. The Haganah (the Jewish defence militia) and the two Jewish extremist groups, the Stern Gang and the Irgun Zvai Leumi, launched an offensive in early 1948 aimed at consolidating their control over the territory allocated to the Jewish State and seizing certain key areas from the proposed Arab State. The Jews were well-armed and well-organized. The Palestinians, in contrast, possessed few weapons, since Britain had never allowed them to re-arm after the great Revolt of 1936-8. Their leaders were still in exile; those who remained were divided among themselves and totally unprepared. Thousands of Arabs were already fleeing to the neighbouring Arab countries either after being driven from their homes or simply to escape the fighting.

On 15 May 1948, the British Mandate expired, and the last British troops departed. Britain did not hand over authority to anyone. The Jews proclaimed the new State of Israel,

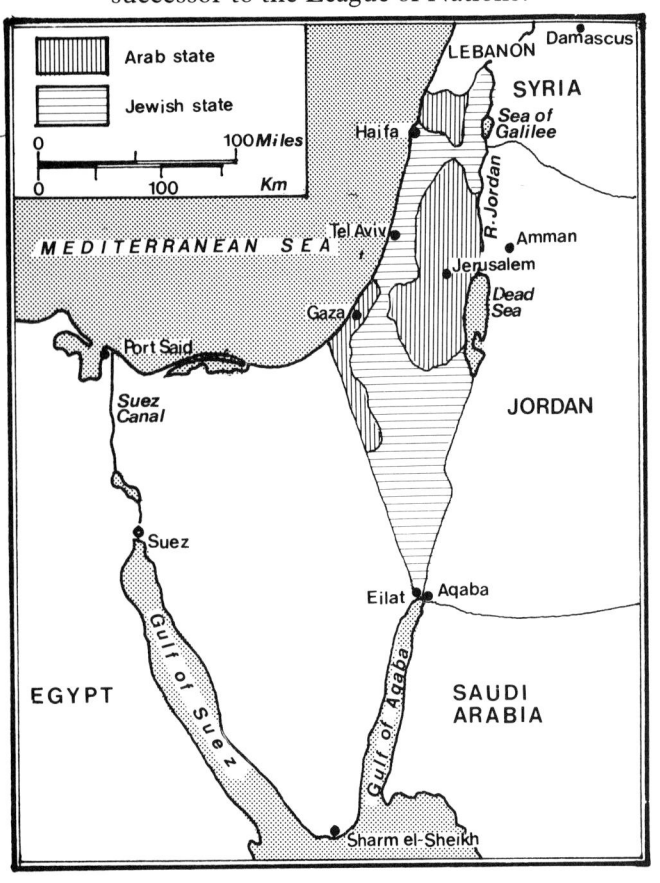

1 The UN plan for the partition of Palestine, 1947.

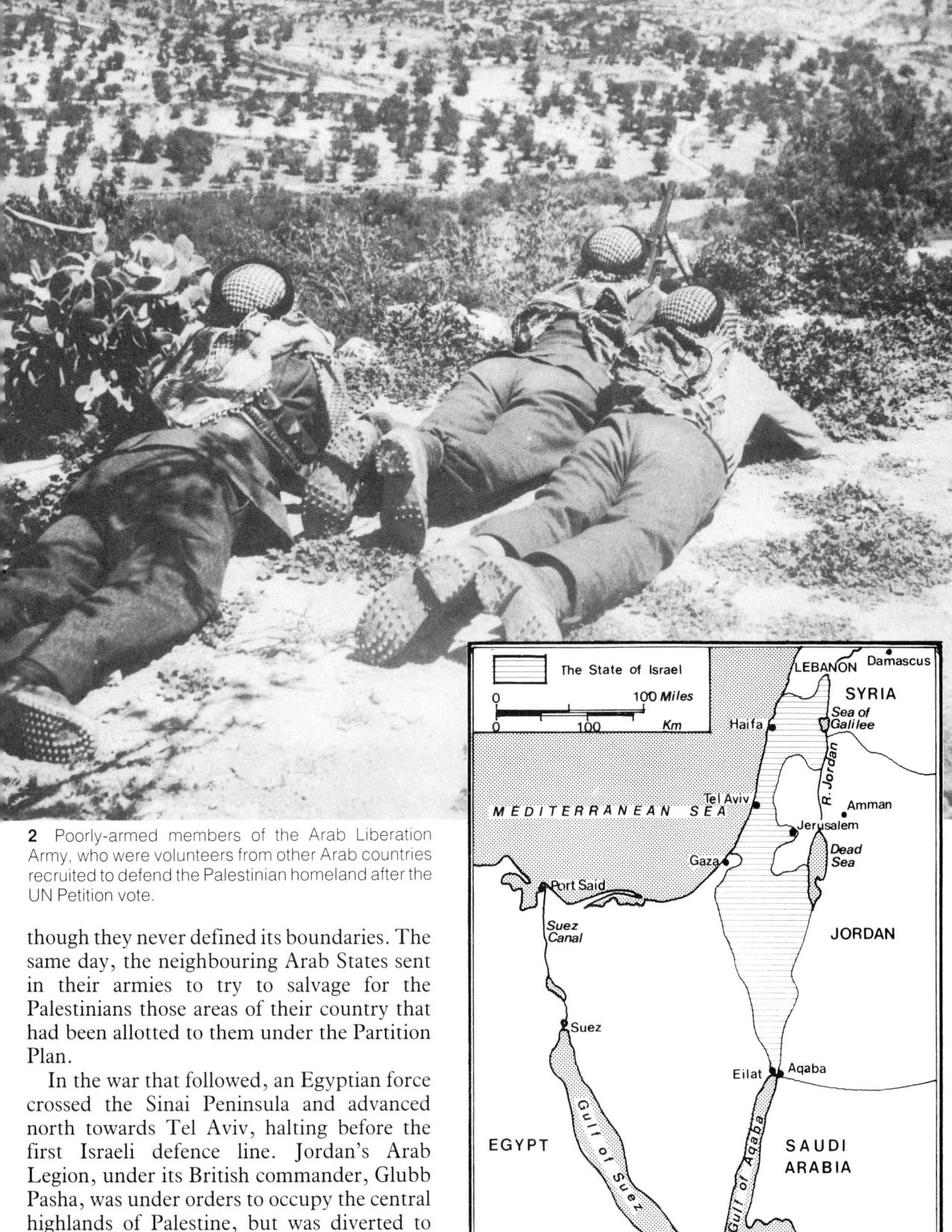

2 Poorly-armed members of the Arab Liberation Army, who were volunteers from other Arab countries recruited to defend the Palestinian homeland after the UN Petition vote.

though they never defined its boundaries. The same day, the neighbouring Arab States sent in their armies to try to salvage for the Palestinians those areas of their country that had been allotted to them under the Partition Plan.

In the war that followed, an Egyptian force crossed the Sinai Peninsula and advanced north towards Tel Aviv, halting before the first Israeli defence line. Jordan's Arab Legion, under its British commander, Glubb Pasha, was under orders to occupy the central highlands of Palestine, but was diverted to

3 The State of Israel after the 1948 war.

protect the Old City of Jerusalem from an Israeli attack. On 11 June 1948, a United Nations truce came into effect for four weeks. During this time, Israel received large quantities of much-needed reinforcements including aircraft, light and heavy arms and volunteers from abroad. When the truce expired, Israel was ready to fight the next round in its battle for survival. The Arab armies, in contrast, were weakened by shortages of arms and ammunition and were seriously divided among themselves. Egypt and Jordan were extremely suspicious of each other's ambitions, and there was no agreement between them about objectives. When the second phase of the war ended in July, the Arabs held only the central highlands and a narrow coastal strip around Gaza. Jerusalem was divided: the Old City remained under Jordanian control and the newer suburbs were incorporated in the new state of Israel. A series of armistice agreements were concluded in Rhodes during 1949 between Israel and the neighbouring Arab states: Egypt, Lebanon, Jordan and Syria. The Jewish state ended the war with considerably expanded borders. It now controlled over 77 per cent of Palestine, rather than the 57 per cent allotted to it under the UN Partition Plan.

The Arab state of Palestine never came into being. The central highlands, which were under Jordanian military control, were annexed in 1950 by King Abdullah (pp. 27-31) and became known as the West Bank of the Kingdom of Jordan. The Egyptians, whose army controlled the Gaza Strip, set up an "All Palestine Government" under the Mufti of Jerusalem, who had led Palestinian opposition to the British. But it never acquired any degree of authority and soon disappeared into oblivion. The Palestinian people were scattered and divided, with neither control over their political future nor voice of their own. Some 800,000 had become refugees, having fled or been driven from their homes in the area occupied by the State of Israel. Those who remained were placed under military rule. Very few were ever allowed to return. The dispossession and statelessness of the Palestinians since 1948 has prevented the conclusion of any lasting peace in the area. The armistice agreements established only an unsteady truce between Israel and her neighbours.

The defeat of the Arab armies in the war in 1948 discredited the old regimes and contributed to political and economic upheaval in the Arab world. The establishment of the new state of Israel in the Arab heartland and the closing of its borders cut off traditional markets, supplies and trading routes in the region. Syria and Jordan experienced severe economic problems, which were aggravated, particularly in the case of Jordan, by the huge numbers of destitute Palestinian refugees. The Arab countries had themselves only recently achieved independence from Britain and France and faced profound domestic problems.

Syria suffered a number of military coups in the years after the war and remained politically unstable throughout the 1950s and 1960s. King Abdullah of Jordan was assassinated in 1951 but was succeeded in an orderly fashion first by his son and then by his grandson, Husain. In Egypt, King Farouk was deposed by the Free Officers, who staged a military coup in 1952. In 1954, one of these officers, Gamal Abdul Nasser (pp. 31-35), became President of Egypt. He became the champion of Arab nationalism and was soon acknowledged as leader of the Arab world by the Arab masses everywhere.

Both the Arab states and Israel were preoccupied with domestic problems after 1949, but the lack of peace led them increasingly into an arms race in the years following the first Arab-Israeli war. The Arab states, like the Palestinians themselves, regarded the dispossession of the original inhabitants of Palestine as a fundamental injustice, but they were not strong enough to do anything about it. The Palestinian refugees frequently crossed the borders into Israel to salvage what possessions they could, to harvest the crops on their own lands, to return home or to exact revenge. Israeli troops generally shot these "infiltrators" on sight, and cross-border raids by both sides raised

4 Dr Chaim Weizmann, seen here taking the oath as first President of Israel on 16 February 1949.

tensions and fuelled the arms race. A particularly savage, unprovoked, attack on Egyptian troops in Gaza by the Israelis in February 1955 caused an outcry in Egypt. Nasser could no longer afford to ignore his army's demands for weapons and, later that year, he concluded a large arms deal with Czechoslovakia.

This led directly to war in 1956. The arms deal alarmed Israel, and Nasser's nationalization of the Suez Canal Company enraged Britain and France (pp. 43-46). On 29 October 1956, Israel invaded Sinai and two days later Britain and France carried out air raids on Egypt and landed troops at Port Said at the entrance to the Suez Canal. World opinion was appalled at this blatant aggression. Under strong pressure from President Eisenhower of the United States, Britain backed down. British and French troops were evacuated and the Israelis forced to withdraw from the Sinai Peninsula and the Gaza Strip.

The arms race between Israel and the Arab states continued apace. As a result of the war in 1956, a United Nations Emergency Force (UNEF) was stationed on the border between Israel and Egypt and at key points in the Sinai Peninsula. Israel adamantly refused to have UN troops stationed on Israeli territory, so they were only stationed on the Egyptian side. Cross-border attacks and massive Israeli reprisal raids continued and were one of the major causes of the outbreak of full-scale war in 1967, as they had been in 1956.

In 1966, yet another coup in Syria brought to power a radical, militantly anti-Zionist government. It established close ties with the USSR and began to receive Soviet arms supplies. It also encouraged the Palestinian guerrilla movements to mount cross-border raids into Israel. The Israeli government threatened to punish Syria, and a nervous Syrian government asked Nasser for support.

Anxious to rebuild his crumbling prestige as leader of the Arab world, Nasser felt he could not afford to sit idly by while Syria was at risk. He proceeded to make a series of hostile gestures: he moved troops towards the Israeli border, asked for the withdrawal of UNEF and announced that the Straits of Tiran (at the entrance to the Gulf of Aqaba) were closed to Israeli shipping. The Israelis regarded this last act as a declaration of war. On 5 June 1967 they destroyed Nasser's airforce in a devastating aerial attack and invaded the Sinai Peninsula. Syria and Jordan joined in the war, believing from Cairo Radio's broadcasts on the morning of 5 June that Israel was facing defeat. By the end of the Six-Day War, as it became known, Israel had made substantial territorial gains, occupying the rest of Palestine (the West Bank and the Gaza Strip), the Egyptian Sinai Peninsula and the Syrian Golan Heights.

The Six-Day War was a great victory for Israel and a devastating defeat for the Arabs. For the Palestinians, it was nearly as great a disaster as 1948 had been. Some 355,000 fled from the West Bank during and after the war. Many of these people were refugees from 1948 and were now uprooted for the second time in their lives. Only about 14,000 were allowed to return to their homes. Israel at once set about consolidating its hold on the occupied territories, and the Arab states refused to negotiate a peace that would leave Israel to enjoy the benefits of its victories. They preferred defiance and started rebuilding their armies for the next war. There was still no

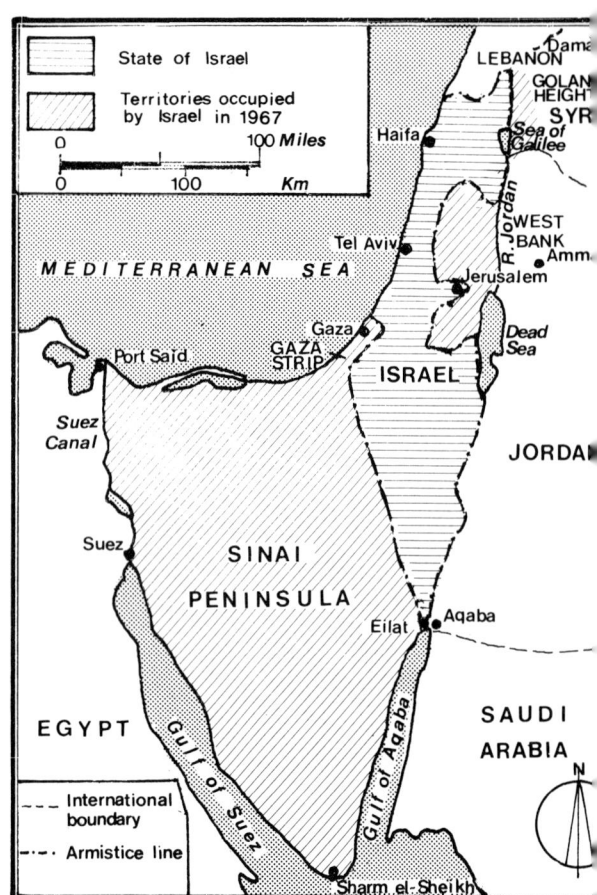

5 Territories occupied by Israel in the 1967 war.

lasting peace, though in the moment of their victory, the Israelis did not believe that it mattered. They felt secure in the strength of their armed forces. Nevertheless, the problem of the dispossessed Palestinians remained unresolved. By occupying the remainder of historical Palestine, Israel brought under its rule over one million Arabs who included among their number many who were refugees from the 1948 war. In this way, the Palestinian problem was brought home to Israel. The Arab states shifted their immediate attention away from trying to right the wrong done to the Palestinians toward trying to recover the territories lost in the 1967 war. The Arab-Israeli struggle entered a new phase.

ZIONISTS

The Zionist movement appeared in Europe in the late nineteenth century. It grew in strength in Eastern Europe in particular as a result of the persecution of the large Jewish communities there. It was also influenced by contemporary nationalist ideas. The ideal of early Zionist groups was to return to Palestine and redeem the land of the Jewish people, where they would be able to live in security. The First Zionist Congress was held in Basle in 1897 and Theodor Herzl, regarded as the founder of political Zionism, boasted afterwards that at Basle he had founded the Jewish State. The Zionists believed that only by drawing all Jews together into a Jewish State would they be able to live a "normal" existence like other nations and be free from the fear of hostility and discrimination. They were convinced that anti-Semitism was inevitable and endemic in other societies, and that only by removing themselves to a state of their own would they ever be free from it.

Zionism was born in Europe and attracted little interest elsewhere in the world until the Second World War. Jews elsewhere had not had the same historical experience. Even in Europe, many Jews were hostile to the idea, either because it contradicted their religious beliefs concerning the coming of the Messiah and the Return or because they feared they would be accused of disloyalty to the countries in which they were living. Most Zionists were not at all religious. They were strongly attached to their Jewish identity but they wanted to build a secular state. The adoption of Hebrew, the sacred language, for daily life and communication was a step that offended some religious people, but for Zionists it represented an important stage in the creation of a new Jewish society and culture.

The First Zionist Congress declared that "Zionism strives to create for the Jewish People a home in Palestine secured by Public Law". But Zionist appeals to the Sultan of

6 Theodor Herzl, founder of the World Zionist Organization.

Turkey, Abdul Hamid II, for permission to settle there were refused. The Sultan did not want trouble among his subjects, and the Arabs living in Palestine were alarmed by the establishment of foreign Zionist colonies. The Zionists, for the most part, blithely ignored the fact that the land was already occupied. They did not really think about the Arab inhabitants any more than the European empires thought about the native peoples of the lands they ruled. Later, the problem of relations with the Arabs in Palestine became rather more urgent, and Zionist leaders differed in their responses to it.

Herzl realized that the Zionists would have to obtain the support of one of the Great

Powers if they were to have any chance of success. Germany took up the cause for many years but it failed to persuade the Ottoman Sultan to change his mind. When the British government issued the Balfour Declaration in 1917, it was rightly regarded by the Zionists as a major breakthrough.

Under the terms of the Mandate, the Jewish Agency for Palestine was established. It was supposed to advise and co-operate with the British Administration in Palestine on matters affecting the Jewish National Home and take part in the development of the country. It rapidly became a state within a state, working towards its goal of transforming Palestine into an exclusively Jewish state. It encouraged large-scale Jewish immigration into the country, which had previously been overwhelmingly Arab in population. The Jewish population rose from 8 per cent of the total in 1918 to about 30 per cent by the end of the Second World War. The rise of Nazi Germany and the persecution of Jews by Hitler's regime had a dramatic effect on the Zionist programme. Jewish immigration to Palestine had tailed off in the 1920s, but in the 1930s Jews fleeing from the Nazi Holocaust in Europe arrived in large numbers. The Zionists could not hope to create a Jewish state in Palestine when the Jews living there were so outnumbered by the Palestinian Arabs. But by the close of the Second World War the dream of the Jewish state was almost within their grasp.

David Ben-Gurion (1886-1973)

David Ben-Gurion was born as David Yosef Gruen at Plonsk in Poland on 16 October 1886. Early in his youth he was attracted by Zionism: "It was from my father that I inherited my love for the Land of Israel . . . and for the Hebrew language". He joined the Po'alei Zion (Workers of Zion) and in 1906 emigrated to Palestine, where he worked as a farm labourer in Jewish settlements.

He took the Hebrew name of Ben-Gurion while working in Jerusalem in 1910 and he became active in the labour movement in the Yishuv (the Jewish community in Palestine). He was exiled from Palestine by the Ottomans in 1915 because his Zionist politics were deemed to be hostile "to the interests of the Turkish Empire". In 1918 he helped to raise a Jewish Legion in the United States and served in it under General Allenby in the Palestine campaign.

The defeat of Turkey in the First World War changed the future of Palestine. Ben-Gurion regarded the Balfour Declaration as a miracle:

The greatest state in the world has announced its official recognition of the existence of a Hebrew nation, and has committed itself to aid in the establishment of a National Home in Palestine.

Ben-Gurion soon rose to the top of the Jewish institutions in Palestine between the two World Wars. In 1930, he became leader of the Mapai (Labour) party, one of the political groupings that emerged within the Yishuv. In 1935, he became Chairman of the Executive of the Jewish Agency in Palestine, which effectively governed the Jewish Community there under the British Mandatory authorities.

By the time the Second World War broke out, it was clear to everyone that the aspirations of the Zionists in Palestine conflicted with those of the Palestinian Arabs and that a clash was inevitable. The Jews had assisted the British in crushing the Arab rebellion in Palestine in 1936-8, but the rebellion and the threat of war with Germany led the British to change their policy. The 1939 White Paper declared that only 75,000 more Jews would be allowed to enter Palestine during the next five years; after that the establishment of self-rule would effectively preserve the Arab majority in the country. The British, who had once been friends, now became the enemies of the Zionists. But, faced with the Nazi threat, Ben-Gurion decided that the Zionists must support the Allies in the war until the Germans were defeated.

In 1941, Ben-Gurion toured the world to expound his views of the future. He visited Cambridge, where William Frankel was one of the two students assigned by the London Zionist HQ to act as local guides. Frankel recalls the speech Ben-Gurion gave to a meeting with some Jewish lecturers and undergraduates there:

The Jewish people, he declaimed, would have a Jewish State in Palestine when the war ended. But nobody should for one moment assume that it was going to be handed up on a plate by the British Government. The Jews would have to fight for it; there would be a bitter struggle and blood would flow. . . .

I doubt that anyone had propounded the Zionist programme in these terms in Cambridge before. The audience was both electrified and depressed. As I was helping one don on with his coat on the way out, he muttered: "If that's the leader of the Jews of Palestine, then God help them". (*The Guardian* 21/3/87)

During the Second World War, Ben-Gurion busied himself with preparations for war with the Arabs. He co-operated with the British authorities in the fight against the Germans, and Jewish forces gained valuable military experience in the process. These forces, the Haganah, later formed the nucleus of the regular Israeli army. He dissociated himself from the Jewish extremists – the Irgun Zvai Leumi and the Stern Gang – but he knew that they helped to put pressure on the British Administration, and so the Jewish Agency took no action against them. As soon as the war was over, the British authorities came under attack, because they stood in the way of the creation of a Jewish state in Palestine.

In 1947, the British gave up the struggle to govern Palestine. They announced that they would hand back the Mandate, and withdraw their troops and administration from Palestine. During the course of that summer, Ben-Gurion became convinced that neither the Zionist movement, nor the Jewish community in Palestine, nor the Haganah realized the gravity of the dangers ahead.

There's going to be a war. The Arab countries will unite and. . . there will be battlefronts. This

7 David Ben-Gurion, proclaiming the birth of the Jewish state, 14 May 1948.

will no longer be a war of platoons or sections. It is essential to set up a modern army. It is essential to think of the requirements of a modern army.

By October 1947, when the Arab press was talking of war against the Jews, Ben-Gurion had already stepped up orders to purchase weapons. He also made some important strategic decisions. No Jewish settlement would be abandoned, even if it was in the area that might be allocated to an Arab state. This meant that Haganah forces would be dispersed about the country. If the partition boundaries were not to the liking of the Zionist leadership, the Jews would attempt to extend the borders of the Jewish state.

On 14 May 1948, the day before the British Mandate expired, Ben-Gurion chaired a meeting of the People's Council, read out the Declaration of Independence, and assumed the office of Prime Minister and Minister of Defence of the Provisional Government of Israel.

On 15 May, the armies of the Arab states invaded Palestine but the arms and planes that were on their way to Israel had yet to arrive. The first few days were anxious ones. But the Arabs failed to break through the Jewish lines, and the planes arrived from Czechoslovakia, and then a shipload of arms. By 24 May, Ben-Gurion was confident enough to present his strategic aims to his General Staff:

I proposed that, as soon as we received the equipment on the ship, we should prepare to go over to the offensive with the aim of smashing Lebanon, Transjordan and Syria... If Egypt still dares to fight on, we shall bomb Port Said, Alexandria, and Cairo... And in this fashion, we will end the war and settle our forefathers' accounts with Egypt, Assyria, and Aram.

Ben-Gurion thought in terms of history: the passage of two thousand years was nothing.

Further arms received during the four-week truce in June turned the war decisively in Israel's favour. During the renewed fighting which followed, Israel made significant territorial gains, and armistice agreements were signed in July 1949. The War of Independence was at an end. Bar-Zohar records that Ben-Gurion was asked shortly afterwards why he hadn't "liberated" the whole of Palestine:

The Old Man replied: "There was a danger of getting saddled with a hostile Arab majority... of entanglements with the United Nations and the Powers, and of the State Treasury collapsing. Even so, we liberated a very large area, much more than we thought. Now, we have work for two or three generations. As for the rest – we'll see later..."

It was Ben-Gurion who took many of the decisions that dictated the character of the new Israeli state: The Arabs would be driven out, and never allowed to return, and Jewish immigration would be encouraged as much as possible to build up a strong Jewish majority. Ben-Gurion wrote in his history of the creation of Israel: "To maintain the Status Quo will not do. We have set up a dynamic State, bent upon creation and reform, building and expansion". Ben-Gurion knew that such a course would mean that the Palestinians and the Arab states would not make peace with the new state of Israel, but "If we cannot get real peace for ten or twenty years, we can stand it, and there will be some blessing in it". The threat from outside would help to consolidate the new state, and force the thousands of new Jewish immigrants to work together. But he knew that the Arabs would not always remain weak. Israel needed to be assured of its strength to deter them from attacking to regain their lost land and their rights. Avi Shlaim, an Israeli scholar, remarks

"Ben-Gurion had surprisingly little knowledge or understanding of the Arabs and their culture and no empathy whatever for them... Only by the repeated and vigorous application of force, he concluded, could Israel demonstrate its invincibility and, in the long run, compel the Arabs to come to terms with her existence as an independent sovereign state in the Middle East."

Not all his colleagues agreed with his belligerent plans – his Foreign Minister, Moshe Sharett, was against attacking Egypt in 1956. But Ben-Gurion and Dayan, his Chief of Staff, wanted to strike at Nasser before new weaponry secured in an arms deal with the Soviet bloc strengthened Egypt's armed forces. Israel agreed to launch a joint attack with France on Egypt in return for massive supplies of sophisticated military equipment. When Nasser nationalized the Suez Canal Company in July 1956 the British also entered into this secret agreement. On the 29 October 1956 Israel invaded Egypt and in a lightening campaign, conquered the whole of the Sinai Peninsula, while the British and French carried out air raids on Egypt, and landed paratroops. But there was an international outcry and the Americans forced the Israelis to withdraw from Sinai to their old boundary. Ben-Gurion had misjudged the international climate and for once was compelled to give territory back.

Ben-Gurion's departure from office came about largely through his domineering and unforgiving nature. In the '60s, his methods became increasingly dictatorial, and in the end lost him support. Opposition to his leadership grew and he resigned in 1963, retiring to a kibbutz, Sdeh Boker, in the Negev.

There was popular demand for his return to the premiership on the eve of the Six-Day War in 1967, but his misjudgement of Israel's strength – he was against starting hostilities – showed that he was out of touch.

After the war, he began to withdraw from the political scene. He died on 1 December 1973, just after Israel's next war with her Arab neighbours.

In the historical memory of Israel, he remains the father of the State and the expression of a national consensus never more united and purposeful than when he was its undisputed leader. (*William Frankel*)

8 Ben-Gurion, welcoming Israeli troops on the Dome of the Rock in Jerusalem on 8 June 1967 during the Six-Day War.

Menachem Begin (1913-   )

Throughout his political career, Menachem Begin represented the uncompromising Zionist hard-liners, whereas Ben-Gurion dealt in practical possibilities. They shared the Zionist ideal of a Jewish state, but their political affiliations were totally opposed.

Menachem Wolfovitch Begin was born on 16 August 1913 in Brest-Litovsk, Poland. His father was a committed religious Zionist and sent his son to a school where the tuition was entirely in Hebrew, although the family spoke Yiddish at home. Menachem studied law at Warsaw University and was active in the right-wing Zionist youth organization, the Betar, of which he soon became one of the leading figures.

In 1939 the Nazis invaded and overran Poland and Begin fled to the USSR, where the Russian security police imprisoned him. He was released in 1941, enlisted in the Free Polish Army and was sent to British-mandated Palestine, where he arrived in 1942. The Labour Party, led by Ben-Gurion, controlled the Jewish Agency and the Jewish forces of the Haganah in Palestine. Begin was asked by the underground Irgun Zvai Leumi (National Military Organization) to take charge of its organization in Palestine and did so as soon as he was discharged from the Army in December 1943.

The Irgun had split away from the mainstream Labour Zionists led by Ben-Gurion and carried out terrorist acts against the Palestinian Arabs. By the time Begin arrived in Palestine, the Irgun itself had split and the Stern Gang, a small group, was operating on its own. Begin at once started to build up the Irgun, and on 1 February 1944 declared a revolt against British rule. Their attacks on British installations were intended to lead to British withdrawal from Palestine and the subsequent conquest of the whole of Palestine (which in their view included Jordan as well) by the Jews.

Begin's revolt achieved little during the war years, but after the war the combined operations of the Haganah and the Irgun persuaded Britain to abandon Palestine. On 29 June 1946, the Irgun blew up the King David Hotel, which housed the British Military and Civilian Headquarters in Jerusalem. Over 100 people were killed. Although the Haganah had approved this operation and warnings were given, the Jewish Agency rushed to denounce the attack when the loss of life became known. But while the Jewish Agency disowned and condemned the Irgun's terrorist operations, it made no effort to put a stop to them. They helped to put pressure on the British to leave. Throughout Palestine, Menachem Begin was hunted by the police as a terrorist. Begin denounced the UN Partition Resolution of 1947 as "an illegal act":

to the rest of the world, partition looked like a Zionist victory; to Begin it was only a step towards victory. It galvanized Zionism, but an Israel without a Jerusalem is no Zionist state. The World Zionist Organization leadership had given away most of the biblical patrimony, it was up to the Irgun to make sure that they did not retreat further and to win more of the homeland. (Lenni Brenner in *The Iron Wall*)

The violence started after the UN vote; the Arabs attacked the Jews, and the Jews responded with vigour. If the Arabs attacked Jews, Begin wrote in his memoirs, "we would smite them hip and thigh". As before, bombs were placed by the Irgun in Arab cafes, in the market place in Haifa and in front of the Damascus Gate in Jerusalem. Britain announced it was leaving, and the UN started to reconsider partition.

On 9 April 1948 the Irgun descended on Deir Yassin, a little village on the western outskirts of Jerusalem and brutally massacred its Arab inhabitants. In his memoirs *The Revolt*, Begin justified these actions:

9 The King David Hotel, after the explosion carried out by the Irgun as part of its campaign against the British.

Out of evil, however, good came. This Arab propaganda spread a legend of terror amongst Arabs and Arab troops, who were seized with panic at the mention of Irgun soldiers. The legend was worth half a dozen battalions to the forces of Israel.

Irgun attacks continued. On 25 April 1948, they poured hundreds of shells onto the beleaguered Arab town of Jaffa. After initial resistance the Palestinian Arabs started to flee. What had happened at Deir Yassin had frightened Arabs throughout the country. According to Begin:

There appear to have been two causes for this epidemic flight. One was the name of their attackers and the repute which propaganda had bestowed on them . . . The second was the weight of our bombardment . . . Yigal Yadin, Operations Officer of the Haganah, told me afterwards that we had not been sufficiently economical with our precious shells. (*The Revolt*)

By the time the armistice agreements were signed between Israel and the neighbouring Arab states, only a small fraction remained of the Arab population who had previously been living in areas occupied by the new Jewish state.

On 14 May 1948, the State of Israel was

15

10 The arms ship Altalena, with its cargo of 5000 rifles and 250 machine-guns destined for Begin's Irgun movement.

11 Menachem Begin, campaigning in Haifa in 1950.

12 Jewish immigrants from Europe arriving at Haifa. The Zionist organizations encouraged Jewish immigration in order to build up the numbers of Jews in Palestine.

proclaimed as the British Mandate expired. The Arab armies invaded Palestine, and there was fighting all over the country. On 31 May the Haganah militia was established as a regular army called the Israeli Defence Forces (IDF), and the Irgun agreed to merge into the IDF over the following weeks. A stalemate was reached on all fronts by early June, and on 11 June a truce came into force. It had been arranged by the UN Special Mediator for Palestine, Count Bernadotte (pp. 39-43). On the same day, the *Altalena*, loaded with arms and fighting men for the Irgun, set sail from France. Begin claimed that he did not know the ship had left, but that he immediately tried to recall it to port, since he did not want to take responsibility for breaking the truce.

On 20 June the *Altalena* arrived off the coast of Israel. Ben-Gurion notified Begin that the Provisional Government of Israel would not assume any responsibility for the unloading of the arms, and the IDF told Begin that he must immediately turn over the weapons or the government would use force. Ben-Gurion would not tolerate the Irgun operating outside his control. The subsequent destruction of the *Altalena* off Tel Aviv by the IDF meant the end of the Irgun as an independent organization in the Jewish state.

In October 1948, Menachem Begin announced the formation of a new political party, the Tnuat Ha-Herut (Freedom Movement), to continue the struggle against both the Arabs and the Labour Zionists. The central plank of its platform was the declaration that the Jewish homeland lay on both sides of the Jordan River. Although Begin was elected to the first three Israeli Parliaments, he remained very much an outsider in a Labour-dominated establishment. He applauded the Israeli attack on Egypt in 1956 but he condemned Ben-Gurion for withdrawing from Sinai and the Gaza Strip, areas that the Israelis had conquered in the war. He argued that no part of Eretz Israel (the Land of Israel) should ever be given up. He was a member of the Cabinet that voted for war against Nasser in 1967.

Moshe Dayan (1915-81)

In contrast with Ben-Gurion and Begin, Moshe Dayan represented the new breed of Zionist. He was born and brought up in Palestine, and had never lived anywhere else. In his time, he came to be seen as the archetypal Israeli – a dashing, successful, soldier.

Moshe Dayan was born on 4 May 1915 in Deganiah, a small settlement of Jewish pioneers from Russia in the Jordan valley. He recalled in his memoirs:

I grew up in an independent Jewish society that spoke Hebrew and fostered the values of Israeli Jews who had struck roots and were living in their ancient homeland.

Unlike the European Zionists, however, Dayan made the acquaintance of Arabs in Palestine and spoke Arabic. He always regarded the Arabs as human beings and understood why they opposed the Zionists. Yet he had no hesitation in fighting them. In his military career, like his mentor, Ben-Gurion, he always favoured an activist policy against the Arabs.

He joined the Haganah when he was in his early teens and, during the Arab revolt in 1936, he served with Orde Wingate's British troops crushing the Arab rebellion.

In 1939, Dayan was imprisoned by the British authorities for possessing illegal arms and sentenced to ten years' imprisonment, but two years later he was freed in order to help British forces fighting Germany's allies in Syria and Lebanon. During a battle at the Litani river in Lebanon, he lost his left eye. After this he wore the black eye-patch for which he became so famous. He served as a liaison officer with the British in Jerusalem until 1944, when he returned to farming.

When war broke out between Jews and Arabs after the UN approved the Partition Plan, Dayan at first served in Intelligence. Then, just before the end of the British Mandate in May 1948, he was asked to form a battalion of commando troops. During the war with the Arab states that followed, he commanded on various fronts and led the Israeli troops that captured the towns of Lydda and Ramleh. He was appointed Military Commander of Israeli forces in Jerusalem just before Bernadotte was murdered there by Jewish extremists in September 1948.

In 1949, he served as senior military representative in the Israeli delegation that participated in the armistice negotiations in Rhodes. In that capacity he negotiated the armistice agreement with Jordan, which resulted in important territorial gains for Israel.

He stayed in the army, rising to become chief of operations in Israel in December 1952. He established the infamous Unit 101, which started to carry out brutal reprisal raids across Israel's borders under the command of Ariel Sharon in 1953. Israel's policy of massive reprisals for Palestinian infiltration and

13 General Moshe Dayan (centre) talking to Ben-Gurion (on his right) in Eilat, 1956.

guerrilla attacks contributed to the build-up of tension and ultimately to war in 1956.

Dayan was appointed Chief of Staff in 1953 and master-minded Israel's lightening campaign in the Suez war of 1956, in which Israel conquered the Gaza Strip and the Sinai Peninsula.

In 1957 he left the army to enter politics and became active in the Mapai (Labour) Party, which he had originally joined in 1946. He studied Law and Economics in Tel Aviv University and took courses in Political Science at the Hebrew University in Jerusalem. He was elected to the Knesset in 1959 and made Minister of Agriculture by Ben-Gurion, but quit the Government in 1964, because of differences with Ben-Gurion's successor as Prime Minister, Levi Eshkol.

14 The Israelis overran Gaza and Sinai in a lightening attack on 29 October 1956. Egyptian prisoners are here held under guard in Gaza.

15 Destroyed Egyptian armour and vehicles line the road through the Mitla Pass as they tried to retreat from Sinai in 1967.

Dayan remained a popular military figure with the public, even when out of office. In early 1967, the possibility of war with the Arabs became urgent and threatening. The Prime Minister, Levi Eshkol, was regarded as hesitant and indecisive, but in response to pressure from members of the Knesset and public opinion, he agreed, on 1 June, to appoint Dayan as Minister of Defence even though he was a member of the opposition. Dayan was informed by the Chief of Staff, Yitzhak Rabin, that an initial air strike by Israel was essential for an Israeli victory. At the Ministerial Defence Committee meeting in Jerusalem on Sunday 4 June 1967, Dayan urged that Israel should attack at once:

I believed they [the Egyptians] were anxious to get in the first blow. If they thought that was our intention too, they would not hesitate to beat us to it and launch their attack the day before we did. If they succeeded, the implications for us would be the loss of our advantage of surprise ... we all confidently proclaimed we would win .... Put bluntly, I said, our best chance of victory was to strike the first blow.

The next morning, Monday 5 June 1967, Israel's airforce destroyed two-thirds of Egypt's combat planes in a devastating aerial attack, and effectively assured the Israelis of victory. The Six-Day War was a resounding success for Israel, and though Ben-Gurion was horrified that Dayan had broken the ceasefire in order to attack Syria and conquer the Golan Heights, Israel did not lose Western support as the "Old Man" had feared. In Dayan's words, Israel "ended the Six-Day War with maximum lines on all fronts".

Now Israel was ruling one million Palestinians – in addition to some 300,000 already living in Israel – many of whom were refugees from 1948, still living in refugee camps in the Gaza Strip and on the West Bank. As Minister of Defence, Moshe Dayan was responsible for the military administration of the Occupied Territories and their people.

He took a pragmatic view of the opportunities offered to Israel by the retention of the Occupied Territories, which few Israelis wanted to give up. He at once ordered the barriers and barbed wire that divided Jerusalem to be removed and proclaimed it a united city. He declared a policy of "Open Bridges", which permitted Palestinians from the Occupied Territories to move about freely inside Israel and across the new border into Jordan. These measures offered Israel access to the Arab world through the Occupied Territories and prevented the Palestinians there from being entirely isolated as had been those who had remained in Israel in 1948, and he hoped this would reduce their opposition to Israeli military rule.

Dayan had no illusions about Zionism. Israel had been created by the sword and had to live by it. In 1953, in the course of a funeral oration for a young pioneer killed by Arab guerrillas as he was harvesting grain near the frontier with Egypt, Dayan had said:

Let us not today fling accusations at the murderers. Who are we that we should argue against their hatred? For eight years now they sit in their refugee camps in Gaza, and before their very eyes, we turn into our homestead the land and the villages in which they and their forefathers have lived. We are a generation of settlers, and without the steel helmet and the cannon we cannot plant a tree and build a home. Let us not shrink back when we see the hatred fermenting and filling the lives of hundreds of thousands of Arabs, who sit all around us. Let us not avert our gaze, so that our hand shall not slip. This is the fate of our generation, the choice of our life – to be prepared and armed, strong and tough – or otherwise, the sword will slip from our fist, and our life will be snuffed out.

In June 1967, he was interviewed on "Face the Nation" in the United States. Asked if Israel could absorb the huge number of Arabs whose territory Israel now controlled, he replied:

"Economically we can; but I think that is not in accord with our aims in the future. It would turn Israel into either a binational or poly-Arab-Jewish state instead of the Jewish state, and we want to have a Jewish state. We can absorb them, but it won't be the same country." [Interviewer, Sydney Gruson] "And it is necessary in your opinion to maintain this as a Jewish state and purely a Jewish state?" [Dayan replied] "Absolutely--absolutely. We want a Jewish state like the French have a French state...."

The Arabs accused Dayan's forces of deliberately expelling the refugees who fled during and after the 1987 war. Although the Israeli government denied it, there were persistent reports of intimidation.

Dayan was regarded as a likely successor to Golda Meir as Prime Minister, but his dashing military reputation suffered when Israel was caught out by the Arabs' surprise attack in October 1973.

Arabs

The European colonial empires had been steadily encroaching on the Ottoman Empire's lands during the nineteenth century. France occupied most of North Africa. Britain invaded and occupied Egypt in 1882, and established her influence over the Arab shaikhdoms of the Persian/Arabian Gulf. When the Ottoman Empire was defeated in the First World War, the remaining Arab provinces, which had been expecting independence, found themselves under French and British rule.

The Arab states gradually acquired their independence. Egypt and Iraq signed treaties with Britain during the 1930s, which gave them independence but allowed Britain certain military concessions, and Syria and Lebanon gained full independence in 1946. Jordan officially became independent in 1946, but was so deeply tied to Britain and British advisers that it was refused admittance to the United Nations as an independent state until 1955. Only Palestine was deliberately denied any form of self-rule, since the Arab majority would naturally have opposed Britain's policy of building up a Jewish "National Home" in their country. The Jewish revolt after the Second World War persuaded Britain that it would be better to leave than to attempt to stay on and implement an "unworkable" policy. The "Palestine problem" was handed over to the the UN.

In 1947, the UN Partition Plan recommended the division of Palestine into a Jewish state and an Arab state.

The Arab States had little idea of the military strength of the Zionists in Palestine. They tried to make some sort of common plan of action after the UN vote in favour of Partition, but they could agree on little except condemning the plan. The leaders of the different countries deeply distrusted each other. Most of them were more interested in preventing others from acquiring some of Palestine's territory than in trying to save Palestine for the Palestinians. When they did send in their armies on 15 May 1948, they did not succeed in crushing the new State of Israel or preventing it from annexing land allocated to the proposed Arab state.

The Arabs did not fully realize the serious nature of the danger posed by the Zionists. They underestimated the Zionists' power, determination and influence abroad. The Palestinian leaders were divided, and many had been exiled by the British. Ordinary Palestinians did not know to whom to look for leadership, nor did they know what was in store for them. "We just couldn't believe that the Zionists wanted to chase us away!" An old woman explained to Ingela Bendt and James Downing in *We shall return*, "No, we really didn't. . . .How could they possibly? we thought." She went on to describe their own experience, in their relatively peaceful part of Galilee:

One morning in late May we were working in the fields as usual. . .when bullets suddenly started to explode around us. The Zionists had arrived! They had been hiding outside the village overnight. We ran home, with bullets flying past us, to get our weapons and to ensure that the children were safe. We were completely unprepared for an attack on our area. . .but they were determined to have everything!

The whole society of the Palestinian Arabs was uprooted, and destroyed in 1948. They afterwards referred to the partition simply as the "catastrophe".

Musa Alami (1897-1984)

Musa Alami was one of the few Palestinians who foresaw the possible dimensions of the disaster, but he was unable to prevent it. He was known as a nationalist, but he had no taste for politics, and he later found himself the object of much malicious and harmful suspicion by Palestinian politicians.

As the years of Britain's rule in Palestine drew to an end, Musa found himself an ineffectual bystander as outside forces determined the future of his people and their country. The Palestinians proved themselves unable even to organize a united plan of action.

Musa Alami was born on 8 May 1897 in Jerusalem into one of the most old-established and influential families there. His father, a

16 Musa Alami, a devout Palestinian nationalist who refused to get involved in Palestinian politics.

17 Hajj Amin al-Husseini, Mufti of Jerusalem, the chief Palestinian political opponent to British rule, would not tolerate independent nationalist activities such as those of Musa Alami.

well-to-do Muslim landowner, was an official in the Ottoman administration and eventually became Mayor of Jerusalem. During the First World War, Musa was conscripted into the Turkish army but was branded a deserter for returning late from leave and took refuge in Damascus, where he fell in with the circle of Arab nationalists. After the war, he came to England where he studied law in Cambridge and trained for the bar.

Returning home to Palestine under the British Mandate, he served in the British administration, rising to be the Government Advocate. He became known for his nationalist views, and the Zionists were anxious to get rid of him. In 1937, he was dismissed from his post and sent into exile in

Beirut, where he remained until he was allowed to return to Palestine in 1941.

In spite of his commitment to the nationalist cause, he took no part in Palestinian political life except in a private capacity. But in 1945 the Arab factions in Palestine agreed to send Musa as the Palestine Delegate to the preparatory conference of the Arab League, simply because he was a respected nationalist who belonged to no party and could therefore represent them all. Then whilst running the Arab Office in London, he heard of the British plans to leave Palestine.

Geoffrey Furlonge, in his book *Palestine is my country, the story of Musa Alami*, which is based on Musa's recollections, describes his reaction to this news:

Musa was horrified. A walk-out by Britain, he argued, would be not only a calamity for Palestine, but a moral wrong. She had created the situation in the country, and to abandon it now would be utterly unfair to its people, for whose welfare she bore the responsibility.

Musa Alami returned to Palestine in December 1947. He was alarmed by the contrast between Jewish organization and preparation for the conflict that seemed inevitable and the situation of the Arabs, who were divided and disorganized.

Convinced that the only hope for the Arabs of Palestine would be effective help from the Arab countries when the time came, Musa set off on a tour of the Arab capitals in February 1948 to see what help might be offered.

His first stop, in Damascus, gave him a foretaste of what he was to find everywhere. "I am happy to tell you", the Syrian President assured him, "that our Army and its equipment are of the highest order and well able to deal with a few Jews; and I can tell you in confidence that we even have an atomic bomb"; and seeing Musa's expression of incredulity, he went on, "yes, it was made locally; we fortunately found a very clever fellow, a tinsmith..."

He returned absolutely dejected. He had already seen how strong the Jews had become, and although the Arab armies might be superior in numbers, he doubted that with such leadership and distrust of each other they would be of any help. He concluded that Palestine would be lost.

He left Jerusalem, where bullets were already flying, and spent the next few months in Jordan watching disaster overtake his people.

In the autumn of 1948, he was still under the impression, like the great majority of the Palestinian Arabs, that the division of the country and the exile of most of its people was only temporary.

As he moved among the refugees up and down the Jordan Valley he was assailed from all sides with the one question, "When shall we be able to go home?" But that winter the stark truth of their situation was suddenly thrust upon him. At a reception in Beirut he met a visiting British official, to whom, in all innocence, he posed the same question. He still remembers the shock of incredulity with which he heard the reply, given gently but decisively: that the refugees should think not of returning to their former homes, but of making a new life elsewhere.

Even though experts declared that the refugees could not be resettled in the Jordan Valley, he was not convinced that it would be possible to raise enough money to resettle them elsewhere in the Arab world. In 1949, he applied for permission to enter a tract of wasteland in the Jordan Valley to conduct his own experiments to find water and cultivate the land. He met a good deal of obstruction and resistance. He was not popular with the Jordanian government because he had prevented them requisitioning the Arab Development Society (ADS) funds. His Palestinian enemies spread rumours that he was deliberately aiding Israel by trying to resettle the refugees so that they would give up their tenacious demand to be allowed to return to their old homes.

Nevertheless, he refused to be deflected or discouraged, and obstinately started digging by hand for water, with a few helpers. In January 1950, they found sweet water: they

18 A workshop at Musa Alami's Boys' Camp, where Arab refugees could learn skills.

would be able to live there and cultivate the land. But still a great deal of effort was needed to protect their wells, build houses and raise funds. Musa took in orphaned boys, who were not cared for by the United Nations Relief and Works Agency for Palestine Refugees in the Near East (UNRWA) which was set up in 1950 by the UN to give assistance only to heads of families.

As the project became established, partly with assistance from foreign funds, it was eventually able to house about 50 orphans and give them a limited education and some vocational training, particularly in farming. With these skills they could go out into the world and earn a living. Several generations of young Palestinians were trained in this way.

But the volatile world of Arab politics after the Palestine disaster brought an unexpected calamity in 1955. Musa's Arab enemies took advantage of inflamed emotions in Jordan against the Baghdad Pact and after three days of anti-imperialist agitation in Jericho the leaders of the mobs began to denounce the "nest of traitors and imperialists" at Musa Alami's farm three miles away. The attack was planned with some thought, and about 35,000 men, mostly refugees but with a sprinkling of thugs, approached in seven columns. Musa, by chance, was away in Beirut that day or he would certainly have been killed.

The children were beaten up and everything was destroyed or carried off. At first Musa thought of giving up, but then he realized the boys had no homes to go to. Fired by a sudden cold determination, Musa started anew, with the few faithful helpers who had not deserted him. Things were not easy, but with tireless energy and resolve the project was built up into a bigger enterprise than before. When King Husain was asked to give approval for the funding of a new project, he said:

Musa has not only done all that he says, but he has done more, for he has created hope where no hope was, and therefore we are all behind him.

In June 1967, once again, everything came crashing to the ground, as the Israelis defeated the Arabs and overran Jordan's West Bank. Musa was away in Europe on business. As the Jordanian forces retreated, the countryside was gripped by fear, remembering 1948. Many of the project's staff fled too, and most of the boys disappeared or were fetched away by anxious relatives, till only 35 of the 160 boys and a few staff remained. On 7 June, the first Israeli troops reached the farm. The staff were kept locked up in their houses for five days, till well after the cease-fire had ended the shooting, and the cattle were not fed, watered or milked. Worse, Israeli tanks drove across the fields so laboriously reclaimed from the barren desert, smashed the water-channels and put out of action all but two of the wells. Many of the cattle and chickens were dead or could not be saved.

Once more, with much work and effort, the project was built up again, and, since Musa could not return in the aftermath of the war, he devoted a lot of effort to raising funds and support. By 1968, things were operating again, but the future looked very uncertain, and the obstacles multiplied. His name was mentioned in the Israeli press in a way that implied that the Israeli government was in touch with him. Unwilling to be accused of dealing with the Israelis in any way, he did not at first respond to the invitations to return to Jericho. But later he did resume his work with his Boys' Town in the Jordan Valley – the Arab Development Society's one concrete achievement.

King Abdullah of Jordan (1882-1951)

Abdullah was born in Mecca in February 1882 into a family of ancient and respected lineage with the title of Sharif because they were descendants of the Prophet. He was the second son of Husain al-Hashimi. As a young man, Abdullah spent 16 years of his life in Istanbul, where his father and family were kept partly as guests and partly as prisoners by the Ottoman Sultan, Abdul Hamid, who did not entirely trust them not to make trouble at home. In 1908, however, after the Young Turk revolution, the Ottomans appointed Sharif Husain as ruler of the Hijaz and the family returned to Mecca. Abdullah participated with T.E. Lawrence (the famous Lawrence of Arabia) in the Arab Revolt of 1916 against Turkish rule.

Abdullah was jealous of his younger brother Faisal's sudden rise to prominence as the Arab representative at the Peace Conference at Versailles after the First World War. In 1920, Faisal was elected King of independent Syria but was thrown out by the French, who had been given responsibility for Syria by the League of Nations. The British consoled him by placing him on the throne of British-controlled Iraq. Abdullah meanwhile marched northwards from Mecca in an attempt to win the throne of Syria for himself. But Winston Churchill, the British Colonial Secretary, persuaded him to become ruler of the new state of Transjordan, carved out of the Arab provinces of the defeated Ottoman Empire. Britain had just decided to separate its Mandate for Palestine into two parts, and the area west of the River Jordan became the Emirate of Transjordan. An American scholar, Mary Wilson, described the new Emirate:

Abdullah's domain, as it was created in 1921, had a population of only some 230,000, no real city, no natural resources, and no importance to trade except as a desert thoroughfare. In short, it had no reason to be a state on its own rather than a part of Syria, or of Palestine, or of Saudi Arabia, or of Iraq, except that it better served Britain's interests to be so.

In 1946, Transjordan gained formal independence, but the British still kept their minister at Abdullah's side and their officers in command of his army and they paid a subsidy to keep the country, now called

19 King Abdullah of Jordan at Raghadan Palace in 1948.

simply "Jordan", afloat. So deeply was it still tied to Britain that neither the United States nor the Soviet Union would grant it recognition as an independent state. Abdullah crowned himself King on 25 May 1946. He still nursed ambitions to enlarge his kingdom and become King of Greater Syria. The neighbouring Arab regimes distrusted him and reacted bitterly to his attempts to stir up trouble. The publication of his memoirs in 1945 with its critical and unkind comments about other Arab leaders did not make him any friends.

"There are few people in the Arab states who do not believe that we are instigating Abdullah's activities and when assured that we are not they come back with the assertion that we could stop them if we liked" commented Sir Iltyd Clayton.

The British Minister in Jeddah, Laurence Grafftey-Smith, offered this view in 1946:

. . .I have gathered an impression during the past twenty-five years that King Abdullah is almost universally considered to be no more than a puppet of British policy and a rather bad joke. (Whenever he played chess here at the British Agency, he cheated.)

Abdullah was alarmed by the British decision to get out of Palestine in 1947 as he feared that Britain would abandon the whole area and withdraw his subsidy and their support. Abdullah did not express publicly any support for the UN Partition Plan for Palestine, but went along with the line taken by the other Arab States. In private, however, he urged both London and Washington that the best solution would be partition and the union of Arab Palestine with Jordan under his rule.

Britain was anxiously looking for a policy in Palestine to cover its failure and limit the damage to its interests in the region. It gradually came to the view that, when British forces withdrew in May 1948, Jordan's Arab Legion

if used prudently by King Abdullah in that part of Palestine allotted to the Arab States by the United Nations . . . can do much to prevent the spread of disorder and contribute to the re-establishment of security; indeed it is the only force in sight which is capable of performing these functions

according to a Foreign Office memo in 1948. The British could not afford to be seen to be encouraging Abdullah to annexe the proposed Arab state because they had declared themselves opposed to it. It would be better if Abdullah invaded in collaboration with the other Arab States, and in response to an appeal for help from the Palestinian Arabs.

The Jewish offensive between February and May 1948 roused Arab anger further and increased the commitment of the Arab governments to go to war to protect the Palestinians. The Arab League committed its forces to entering Palestine when the British

20 The Mosque of the Dome of the Rock, in the centre of the picture, built around the Rock of Bayit al Maqdis, from where the Prophet is believed to have made his journey to heaven

left on 15 May. The Arab Legion, staffed by British officers, was the best equipped and trained of all the Arab armies in the field. Abdullah's long-term ambition was to increase the size of his kingdom and embrace his own stature in the Arab world. He was probably the only Arab leader who really knew what he wanted from this campaign; the other Arab states were mostly concerned to prevent him from achieving his territorial ambitions. But he had to be careful because he was militarily and economically dependent on Britain. Sir Alec Kirkbride, the resident British Minister in Amman, informed Abdullah that,

> if Transjordan went beyond the plan regarding the Arab areas of Palestine, His Majesty's Government would doubtless have to reconsider their position regarding the subsidy and the loan of British Officers.

The first campaign of the war lasted about a month. The Arab Legion performed creditably, and Abdullah's standing in the Arab world was raised by its defence of Jerusalem against Jewish attack. During the month's truce arranged by the UN Special Mediator, Count Bernadotte, Abdullah went on a tour of the Arab world, seeking support, but found few friends. Britain, like the United States, had placed an embargo on the delivery of arms to the combatants in Palestine. Now the Arab Legion was running out of ammunition and supplies, and Abdullah felt that Britain, having encouraged him to move into Palestine, was letting him down. "Allies who let one become involved in a war and then cut off our essential supplies are not very desirable friends" he remarked bitterly to Kirkbride.

When the fighting resumed in July, the Arabs were beaten on all fronts. The Jewish forces, strengthened by an inflow of new state of Israel. Although Abdullah could count on some supporters from among the big landowners and traditional local leaders, most of the Palestinian population still regarded him with mistrust. On 1 December 1948, he summoned a conference of Palestinian notables and local leaders at Jericho, where his supporters passed a resolution calling for unification with Jordan. But opposition from the other Arab States and from the British and Americans dissuaded him from declaring it officially. In the meantime, he pursued a policy of "creeping annexation" in his Palestinian territory, and as the lack of alternatives became clearer the Palestinians resigned themselves to the necessity of his rule. One Palestinian explained to the American consul in Jerusalem in 1949:

The officials, the notables, and the people rush forward to kiss His Majesty's hand, when actually many of them would rather break it.

During the Armistice negotiations, and outside them, Abdullah continued to meet the Jewish leaders, hoping to convince them that dividing the old Palestine between themselves would benefit both Israel and Jordan. The Israelis were confident of their military superiority and were extremely demanding. Abdullah made a number of small territorial concessions, hoping for a favourable settlement later, but the Israelis took their gains and then lost interest in offering any settlement in return. Threatened by the Israeli army, Abdullah ceded a strip of territory three miles deep and 40 miles long on the Israeli border. There were 16 villages and 35,000 villagers adversely affected:

When the terms of the armistice were announced riots broke out in the West Bank. The villagers whose lands were suddenly on the Israeli side of the border were especially bitter. They denied Abdullah's right to negotiate over land that was not his, land that they had protected during the war, and they attempted without success to revise the armistice ... Mark Etheridge, the American member of the Palestine Conciliation Commission, said that his

21 General Glubb Pasha, British commander of the Arab Legion, 1941.

arms, pressed home their offensives. The Arab Legion abandoned Lydda and Ramleh to the Israelis and nearly all their inhabitants were expelled towards Jordan. Abdullah's standing fell as dramatically as it had risen earlier with the defence of Jerusalem. There were strikes and angry demonstrations in Jordan and eastern Palestine. Abdullah managed to push most of the blame onto Glubb Pasha, the British commander of the Legion.

Abdullah's army now held the whole of eastern Palestine. This area had doubled in population with the influx of destitute refugees from the lands occupied by the new already difficult task had been made much the more so by "Abdullah selling everything all down the garden".

In March 1950, with the Arab Legion still occupying the West Bank, elections were held in all Abdullah's territories. The new Assembly duly passed an Act of Union of 25 April 1950, incorporating the West Bank into the Kingdom of Jordan.

On Friday 20 July 1951, as Abdullah entered al-Aqsa Mosque in Jerusalem for the noon prayer, a young Palestinian, Mustafa 'Ashu, shot him in the head from a few paces away, killing him instantly. He was succeeded by his eldest son, Talal, who had only recently recovered from a nervous breakdown, and who was deposed within a year in favour of his own son, Abdullah's grandson, Husain.

Gamal Abdul Nasser (1918-70)

Gamal Abdul Nasser was born on 15 January 1918 in Alexandria, where his father worked as a post office clerk. Gamal was the eldest of 11 children. He grew up during Egypt's struggle for national independence from Britain and became involved in nationalist agitation while still at school. He started to study law at Cairo University but then joined the army in 1937, where he soon distinguished himself. He served in the Palestine war of 1948.

In 1949, Nasser founded the Society of Free Officers, a secret underground group within the Egyptian army, to plan for a revolution in Egypt. The Free Officers successfully mounted a coup on 23 July 1952 and sent King Farouk into exile. Nasser had clearly been the strong-man of the new ruling group and in November 1954 he became President of the Republic of Egypt.

His first concern was the ending of foreign occupation and interference in Egypt and in the other Arab countries. In 1954, he successfully negotiated the withdrawal of British troops from the Suez Canal Zone to take place within two years, thus formally ending over 70 years of British occupation. He

22 King Farouk of Egypt, deposed and sent into exile by Nasser in 1952.

23 British military personnel watching a dredger trying to clear a way through the Suez Canal, blocked by sunken ships.

led Arab opposition to the formation of the Baghdad Pact, a system of alliances that he viewed as an attempt to retain Western influence and domination of the Arab world. When this opposition to the Baghdad Pact prevented him obtaining weapons from the West, he turned to the East and in 1955 concluded an arms deal with Czechoslovakia. It was later revealed that the arms were in fact to be supplied by the USSR. His relations with the West deteriorated sharply, and in 1956 the United States and Britain withdrew their offers of financial assistance to build the High Dam at Aswan on the Nile. This was a vitally important project for the Egyptian government. It hoped to use the dam to provide water for irrigation and electric power to develop Egyptian industry. It was regarded as vital for the programme of social and economic development that the revolution wished to implement in Egypt.

On 26 July 1956, Nasser announced that he had nationalized the foreign-owned Suez Canal Company. The revenues from this would be used to finance the High Dam. Mohamed Heikal, editor of the most important newspaper in Egypt, *al-Ahram*, and a close friend of Nasser, describes the significance of this to the Egyptians:

The people went wild with excitement. The Canal had always stood as a monument to the exploitation of Egypt. Thousands of Egyptians had died digging it. The wildest dream of most Egyptians had been that we might not renew the concession when it ran out in 1968. And now Nasser had nationalized it. It belonged to Egypt.

24 Gamal Abdul Nasser visiting Damascus in 1958, the year in which Syria and Egypt united to form the United Arab Republic.

Nasser had feared some sort of retaliation by Britain and France, the owners of the Suez Canal Company. Some diplomatic moves and threats were made by the British and French, but little happened. Then on 29 October 1956, Israeli forces invaded the Sinai Peninsula as previously arranged in a secret agreement with Britain and France. Under the terms of the secret treaty, Britain and France issued an ultimatum demanding that both Egypt and Israel withdraw their forces 10 miles either side of the Canal and allow Anglo-French forces to occupy the Canal Zone. Egypt and Israel were given 12 hours to comply. Nasser naturally refused. Compliance would have meant Egypt withdrawing from the whole of the Sinai Peninsula, her own territory, and letting Israel occupy it, while the British and French occupied the Canal Zone, which was also Egyptian territory. British aircraft started to bomb Egypt. Nasser's army in Sinai was under fierce attack and the Israelis soon reached the Suez Canal. British and French airborne troops landed in the Canal Zone, and a huge invasion force set sail from Britain's Mediterranean bases. But although he did not have the resources to fight all three countries at once, he did not lose his nerve. Reassured by the crowds of Cairo who declared "we shall fight", Nasser blocked the canal by sinking ships at both ends. He was greatly heartened by the world's condemnation of the attack.

The Anglo-French invasion force landed on 5 November, but the next day, the British accepted the cease-fire demanded by the UN and the fighting stopped. It took many more months to secure the evacuation of the British, French and Israeli troops, and agree a political settlement. American pressure proved decisive in all this, but at the end of the day Nasser emerged from the whole affair a nationalist hero at home and, in the Arab world, a stronger leader than before. His own verdict on the Suez affair was:

the meaning of Suez is that there is an end to the methods of the nineteenth century, that it was impossible to use the methods of the nineteenth century in the twentieth century.

In 1958, his prestige and influence was increased by the political union between Syria and Egypt to form the United Arab Republic. On 14 July 1958, an army coup in Iraq swept away the pro-Western regime, and proclaimed the Iraqi revolution. Initially, the new Iraqi leaders turned to Nasser for support. 1958 was Nasser's "year of victory" for Arab nationalism. But the unity of the Arab nations that he hoped would strengthen them all proved difficult to achieve in practice. Syria withdrew from the union with Egypt in 1961.

His differences and rivalries with the other Arab states were partly patched up in 1964, when he hosted the first summit meeting of all Arab heads of state in Cairo. The principal item on the agenda was the need to present a united front against the Israeli threat to divert the headwaters of the River Jordan. This project would have seriously affected the economies of Jordan, Syria and Lebanon.

Tensions with Israel increased when a new round of cross-border raids by Palestinian guerrillas was met by massive Israeli military reprisals. The new revolutionary government of Syria, installed in 1966, encouraged such raids and preached popular warfare against Israel. Although Nasser did not want to be drawn into a war with Israel, he could not

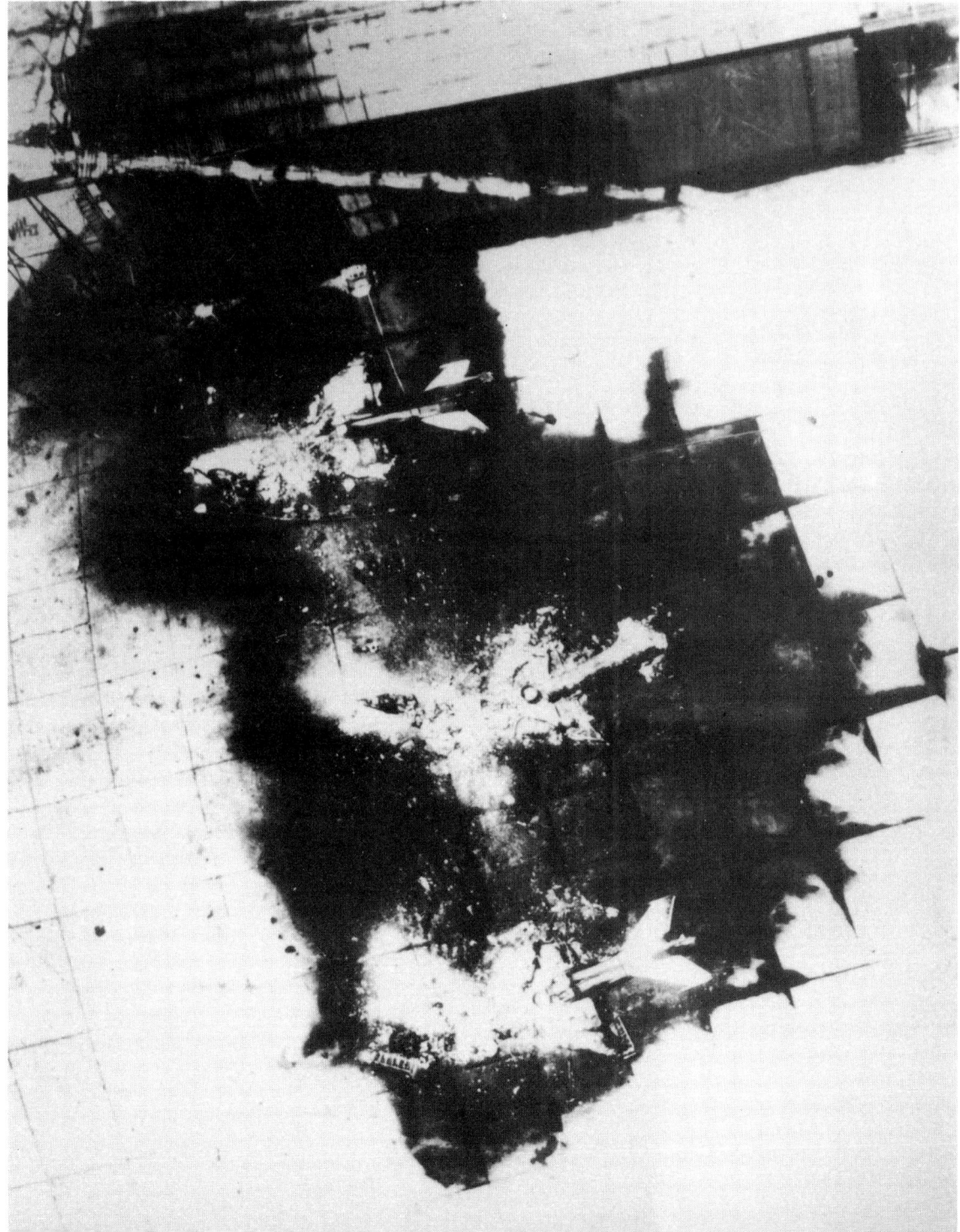

25 Egyptian aircraft destroyed on the ground by Israeli forces in 1967.

afford to stand idly by as the spiral of attack and reprisal grew more dangerous. His prestige as leader of the Arab world and of its single most powerful nation was at stake.

In May 1967, the atmosphere of impending war was heightened. Belligerent threats were broadcast by both sides, and Syria appealed to Nasser for help because it feared an Israeli attack. By his gestures of belligerence, he gave the Israelis the impression of being ready to join an attack against them, and offered them an excuse to strike first. On the morning of 5 June 1967, the Israeli air force, in a massive surprise attack, destroyed 60 per cent of the Egyptian air force on the ground. Without an air force, the Egyptian armies in Sinai were exposed to Israeli air attacks and they withdrew in confusion. Israel now occupied the Sinai Peninsula for the second time. The Six-Day War was a devastating and humiliating defeat for Nasser.

On 9 June, Nasser spoke to the nation over radio and television. He declared that he was ready to assume the entire responsibility for the "setback". He announced that he had decided to give up all his official posts and every political role and become an ordinary citizen. Eric Rouleau, in Cairo as the correspondent of *Le Monde*, vividly described the reaction of the Egyptian people:

In the twilight and the semi-blacked-out streets, hundreds of thousands, some of the men still in pyjamas and the women in nightgowns, came out of their houses weeping and shouting, "Nasser, Nasser, don't leave us, we need you". The noise was like a rising storm. A whole people seemed to be in mourning.

The next day, Nasser withdrew his resignation, and set about rebuilding Egypt's defences and showing its defiance. The Suez Canal remained blocked. The Soviet Union gave arms, equipment and training to rebuild the Egyptian army and air force. Small acts of resistance and bombardments of Israeli positions were carried out to prevent them enjoying their conquests in peace. This "War of Attrition" was to show that Egypt had not surrendered.

Nevertheless, Nasser did not totally recover from this terrible defeat. The repressiveness of the regime increased and so did opposition to it. On 28 September 1970, Nasser died of a heart attack. At his funeral three days later, millions of people poured into Cairo from the countryside and blocked the procession in the streets in an overwhelming expression of grief.

OUTSIDERS

The conflict in Palestine has been influenced by outside powers at every stage in its evolution. Great Britain took up the Zionist cause in the dark days of the First World War. The promises contained in the Balfour Declaration, like the promises made to the Arabs, were given in the hope of obtaining support for Britain's war effort.

During Britain's administration of Palestine between the First and Second World Wars, her material and political support for the Zionist enterprise was crucial. She enabled the Zionists to enter the country and build up self-sufficient institutions governing every aspect of life of the Jewish community there, despite opposition from the Arabs.

When British policy toward the Zionists changed in 1939, it ran into conflict with Zionist ambitions. Ben-Gurion (pp. 10-13) realized the importance of both winning the support of the large and influential Jewish community in the United States and obtaining American support for the principle of a Jewish state in Palestine. As Britain prepared to give up the Palestine Mandate and hand the problem over to the United Nations, the support of America proved decisive. Britain was now a Great Power in decline: America was the new Superpower and carried great weight in the young United Nations Organization.

Western interest in the Middle East was dictated by the existence of the old colonial empires, and, early in the twentieth century, by the discovery of oil. As the Ottoman Empire crumbled, the Western powers hoped to use the Zionists in Palestine to divide and control the Arab provinces. They were motivated by a mixture of sympathy for Zionist aspirations and self-interest. As Zionist ambitions brought them more and more into open conflict with the Arabs so the Western powers tried to reconcile their support for Zionism with the necessity of not antagonizing the Arabs too much. This delicate balancing act was forced upon them because the Arab countries supplied the oil needed for the industrialized Western economies. The disaster in Palestine brought down some of the Arab regimes that had been friendly to the West, and the continuing conflict with Israel threatened Western interests further.

Harry S. Truman (1884-1972)

After the Second World War, the United States was anxious to curb the Soviet Union's growing power and to rebuild a strong Europe in order to do so. There were huge numbers of Displaced Persons and war refugees in Europe who had no homes to go back to. Many would have liked to start new lives in the United States, but the United States was not keen to welcome an enormous influx of impoverished refugees. Zionist agitation over Palestine and the issue of Jewish immigration to the National Home there found ready listeners in America and became an issue in American domestic politics.

Harry Truman took several decisions on the Palestine problem that were influenced more by domestic considerations than foreign policy issues. But they had significant and far-reaching repercussions that profoundly altered the course of events.

In the 1944 Presidential elections, Franklin D. Roosevelt was re-elected President with Harry Truman as his Vice-President. When Roosevelt died in April 1945, Harry Truman succeeded him in office for the rest of his term. He represented in many ways a typical self-made, white, middle-class, 60-year-old American, but as the "everyday American" who became President he had to make some historic decisions.

The summer of 1945 marked President Truman's first intervention in the Palestine problem. He wrote to the British Prime Minister, Winston Churchill, asking him to end all restrictions on Jewish immigration into Palestine. Six weeks later, in August 1945, President Truman sent a letter to Churchill's successor as Prime Minister, Clement Attlee, requesting that the British admit 100,000 Jewish refugees from Europe into Palestine. He had been appalled by the plight of Jewish refugees from the Nazis who were living in Displaced Persons' Camps in Europe at the end of the War in miserable conditions. He wrote that the granting of 100,000 entry certificates of immigration to Palestine would contribute to the solution of the future of the European Jews. To most Americans and to the President himself, the admission of the 100,000 Jewish refugees to Palestine would be a sincere humanitarian act.

The British government was alarmed by this request, for Truman had linked together two issues that had previously been separate: the problem of the Jewish refugees in Europe and the problem of Palestine. The British did not think that the European Jews should be sent to Palestine. It was only a small and rather poor country, and the Europeans would be better off re-building their lives in Europe or in the United States, but the United States was not willing to relax its strict immigration laws to allow large numbers of them in.

Truman had not really mastered the issues at the heart of the Palestine problem and he received conflicting advice and pressure from his officials at the State Department and outside. He resented the pressure and accusations

26 President Truman, on a tour of the United States in the first year of his presidency.

of the Zionists, he was angered by critics who implied that the President was a captive of the New York Jews and he became frustrated when the bureaucratic machinery of government appeared to thwart his humanitarian efforts to relieve the displaced Jews in Europe. 'There are people on the 3rd and 4th levels of the State Department who have always wanted to cut my throat' he wrote in his diary in the spring of 1948.

In November 1947, the United Nations'

27 Clement Attlee on 26 July 1945, the day of Labour's election victory.

vote for the Partition of Palestine hung in the balance and much behind-the-scenes lobbying went on. Truman himself finally threw his weight behind the Zionists – he wrote in his memoirs that he never 'had so much pressure and propaganda aimed at the White House as I had in this instance'. The vote for partition was later described as 'Israel's basic title to independence' by Sumner Welles, who had served in the State Department and was regarded as the foremost non-Jewish champion of Zionism in America.

Truman was concentrating on trying to get himself re-elected in the imminent Presidential elections of 1948. Domestic vote-catching had a part to play in foreign policy decisions because of the large Jewish community in the United States. John Balfour, who was serving as a British diplomat in Washington in 1946, later wrote:

"It is clear that the President himself has always supported partition. Although there is no reason to doubt his personal sincerity, it is also true that he has been under very great pressure from his campaign managers, who have all along been terrified of incurring the ill-will of the very powerful Zionist lobby and of its loyal blocs of voters in key states."

When asked for an explanation of his pro-Jewish policy, Truman himself exclaimed:

'I have to answer to hundreds of thousands who are anxious for the success of Zionism; I do not have hundreds of thousands of Arabs in my constituents'.

But the violence and anger in Palestine after the UN vote caused the Americans to retreat from their support for such a solution. In May 1948, when the British were about to depart from Palestine, American policy shifted from favouring United Nations trusteeship to support for a truce, and then to the prospect of mediation between the two warring sides. On 14 May 1948, the day before the expiry of the British Mandate, the State of Israel was proclaimed. A few minutes after the Mandate expired, Truman declared that the United States recognized the State of Israel. The sudden announcement of recognition threw American policy into disarray. At the moment that it happened, the UN, meeting at Lake Success, was discussing the proposal sponsored by the United States to send a UN Special Mediator to Palestine. The American delegates had worked hard to secure enough votes in favour of it, when they themselves learned of the Presidential proclamation from rumours among the delegates in the session.

In the fighting that followed in Palestine, the new Jewish state succeeded in taking areas that had been allotted to the Arabs under the Partition plan. The UN Mediator, Count Bernadotte (pp. 39-43), produced a provisional plan proposing that the Jews should give up some of areas they were holding. On 21 September 1948, the United States' State Department accepted the Bernadotte plan in its entirety, but, under pressure from Jewish leaders, Truman retracted it. Seven days before the Presidential election, Truman made the following statement:

We approve the claims of the State of Israel to the boundaries set forth in the United Nations' resolution of November 29 [1947] and consider that modifications thereof should be made only if fully acceptable to the State of Israel.

Truman was re-elected President in a surprise victory in November 1948, although in March his candidacy had seemed hopeless.

President Truman was personally close to Chaim Weizmann, the leader of the World Zionist Organization and first President of Israel. Truman now made it official United States policy that any frontier decisions would have to be acceptable to Israel, and in view of the Israelis' military successes against the Arabs in the 1948 war the Israelis were virtually in a position to dictate a settlement. However, Truman expected the Israeli leaders to behave in an internationally acceptable manner, and American tolerance of Israeli ambitions proved to have its limits. Israeli military strikes across the Egyptian frontier provoked a message from President Truman that there might be a "substantial review" of American support unless the Israelis acted in the manner of a "peace-loving state". This mild rebuke had the required effect and produced instantaneous results. The line had been drawn.

Truman did not stand for re-election in 1952. He retired to Independence, Missouri, where he had been educated. He died in 1972.

A Zionist historian paid this tribute: "Truman is incontestably one of the principal architects of the State of Israel".

Count Folke Bernadotte (1895-1948)

Count Folke Bernadotte was born in Stockholm, Sweden on 2 January 1895, a nephew of King Gustavus V. He had deeply held Protestant convictions and a strong sense of public duty. During the Second World War, he had made his name as a representative of the International Red Cross, and, in 1945, had led a Swedish Red Cross delegation to Nazi Germany to evacuate Scandinavian prisoners from the concentration camps. In this work, he had earned the respect of both sides for his integrity and impartiality and had always been granted free access. He had managed to save thousands of Jewish lives by these activities, and his experience of Jewish suffering in Europe led him to lean towards the Jewish side in the conflict in Palestine. In contrast, he knew little or nothing about the Arabs, their culture, their religion or their views on the Palestine problem.

According to his memoirs, published after his death, he laughed when he was first told that he was being considered for the office of United Nations Mediator "in the ugly-looking conflict between Jews and Arabs which had broken out in Palestine a few days previously." He did not think it would come to anything, but he started to consider whether he should undertake this possibly insoluble task. Eventually he decided that:

If – in the event of my being definitely offered the post – I were to refuse it, I should probably reproach myself for the rest of my life because I had not even tried to make any contribution towards clearing up this difficult situation.

28 Count Folke Bernadotte, United Nations Mediator in Palestine in 1948.

Count Bernadotte took up the appointment on 20 May 1948, when the war in Palestine was raging. Accompanied by his advisers and secretaries, he went immediately to the Middle East. The first and most urgent task was to arrange a truce and stop the fighting. After a week of intensive travelling and negotiation, both sides agreed to implement a truce on 11 June. The fighting had reached a temporary stalemate, and both sides needed a breathing space. Bernadotte was greatly cheered by this achievement, although he admitted:

My thoughts also turned at this moment to the future. I realized that the most difficult part of my task probably still lay ahead: that of achieving "a peaceful adjustment of the future of Palestine". The deep gulf between the view-points of the two parties made this a task the difficulty of which I fully and absolutely recognized. The future alone could show whether a happy solution lay within the bounds of possibility.

His mission was hampered by the fact that the Zionists regarded him as "just a stooge of the British", though he certainly was not. However, in spite of his success in saving Jewish lives from the Nazis, the fact that he had had to deal with Heinrich Himmler, one of Hitler's top lieutenants, in the process, turned Jewish feeling against him. Pablo de Azcarate, of the UN mission, described the Mediator in action, in *Mission in Palestine 1948-1952*:

Count Bernadotte's marked predilection for the spectacular and the ostentatious, undoubtedly helped to create a propitious atmosphere in which the personal action of the Mediator . . . could produce the desired result . . . But whatever the external characteristics of his personality and methods, no one could refuse to pay a tribute of admiration and respect to the wholehearted devotion with which he flung himself into his task, or to his impartiality and his fervent desire to accomplish a work of peace and justice in Palestine.

During the truce, he set out on a new round of consultations and discussions in order to work out some proposals for the future which might be acceptable as a starting point for negotiations. The Mediator spoke with the heads of the governments of Egypt, Jordan, Israel, Lebanon, Syria and Iraq, whose armies were engaged in the fighting in Palestine. He also met the Secretary General of the newly created Arab League, Azzam Pasha. But the Palestinian Arabs had no government of their own. With no leadership and with many of their people already refugees in exile, the Palestinians had proclaimed no state and were not consulted by the United Nations Mediator. Bernadotte records meeting only two Palestinians, who were sent as part of the Arab League's delegation to his headquarters in Rhodes in June in 1948.

He noticed that both the Arabs and the Jews were extremely suspicious. They suspected the other side of gaining advantages from the truce that were denied to their own. He was dismayed by the attacks made upon him in the Jewish press:

I recalled what I had said to my assistants on my first visit to Tel-Aviv, when I was acclaimed at the concert I had been invited to: that the friendliness that flowed towards me then would unquestionably turn to suspicion and ill-will if, in my later activities as Mediator, I failed to study primarily the interests of the Jewish party but sought to find an impartial and just solution of the problem.

On 27 June he put forward some draft proposals as a "possible basis for discussion" in accordance with his instructions from the UN "to use his good offices to promote a peaceful adjustment of the future situation of Palestine". He suggested that

Palestine as defined in the original Mandate entrusted to the United Kingdom in 1922, that is, including Transjordan, might form a Union comprising two members, one Arab and one Jewish.

29 Bernadotte was appalled at the large number of Palestinians made homeless refugees by the fighting. Two years later these refugees from Lydda were still living in tents, without proper homes or regular employment in this camp near Jerusalem.

He proposed some boundary changes and emphasized that the refugees resulting from the fighting should be allowed to return to their homes.

The Arab reply was decidedly negative. Bernadotte was a little more optimistic after visiting the Arab leaders: he received a firm impression that some accommodation might be reached. But when the Israeli Provisional Government's official reply was received on 5 July, it was clear that the Jewish side did not feel able to accept his proposals of 27 June.

On 9 July, the truce expired. In the ten days' war that followed, the Jewish forces made further territorial gains, and new areas of Palestine were emptied of their Arab inhabitants. A new truce was agreed on 17 July, but the military situation in Jerusalem was far from quiet. On 26 July, he asked the Israeli Foreign Minister, Moshe Sharett, to allow the destitute refugees to return, but was told that:

the Jewish Government could under present conditions in no circumstances permit the return of Arabs who had fled or been driven from their homes during the war.

In his later Progress report to the UN, he stated his view that:

It would be an offence against the principles of elemental justice if these innocent victims of the conflict were denied the right to return to their homes while Jewish immigrants flow into Palestine, and indeed, at least offer the threat of permanent replacement of the Arab refugees who have been rooted in the land for centuries.

Bernadotte's initial instinctive sympathy for the Jews in Palestine was being eroded as his dealings with them progressed. In a private conversation with Sharett, he warned that the Government of Israel was losing the international goodwill that it had previously

30 Members of the extremist Stern Gang greet Bernadotte in Jerusalem on 10 August 1948 with placards warning him not to ask Israel to give up territory.

enjoyed; "It seemed as though Jewish demands would never cease".

It was my definite impression . . . – that the Jews now felt they had two enemies. The Arabs were still Enemy No.1. But I and the United Nations Observers ran them a close second. The Arabs had given us every possible help, particularly during the second truce. The Jews, on the other hand, constantly tried to put spokes in the wheel and did everything in their power to make our work more difficult.

Indeed, he came to the conclusion that the military successes enjoyed by the Jews during the ten days of war in July "had gone to their heads". They would not entertain any idea that the Arab refugees should be allowed to return to their homes, or that they should yield any territory held by their army. The Mediator's proposals for a settlement ran counter to Israeli plans, and his Truce Supervision Observers prevented the expansion of Israel's borders.

On 17 September 1948 Count Bernadotte was assassinated in Jerusalem by Jewish terrorists from the Stern Gang. The assassins got away, and the Israeli Government said it was unable to find them. However, after international pressure they eventually arrested two leaders of the Gang. One of them, Nathan Yalin-Mor, denounced the UN Mediator at length during his trial: "He stood in the way of Jewish absorption of the Kingdom of Transjordan, as well as the whole of Palestine". In the eyes of the Jewish extremists, he had become Enemy No.1, and they murdered him.

Sir Anthony Eden (1897-1977)

Robert Anthony Eden (known throughout his career by his second name) was born on 12 June 1897 at Windlestone Hall, Bishop Auckland, in County Durham. He was educated at Eton and read Arabic and Persian at Christ Church College, University of Oxford. During the First World War he was awarded the Military Cross. After the war, he entered politics and became Tory MP for Warwick and Leamington in 1923, a seat that he held until his resignation from the premiership in 1957 ended his political career. He served as Foreign Secretary from 1935-8 and again during the Second World War.

From 1945 to 1951 the Labour Party was in power, and Eden served as deputy leader of the opposition. In 1951, when Churchill formed a new government, Eden once again became Foreign Secretary.

He built up a reputation as a successful and patient negotiator, with a number of foreign policy successes to his credit. One of his achievements was a new Anglo-Egyptian treaty in 1954. The new nationalist government in Egypt was anxious to secure the withdrawal of British troops stationed in the Suez Canal Zone. Under the terms of the new treaty Britain agreed to withdraw its forces from the Suez Canal Zone by June 1956. To Britain's military chiefs, the coming of the nuclear age made the retention of expensive overseas bases unnecessary. On 6 April 1955, Eden succeeded Churchill as Prime Minister.

On 26 July 1956, a month after the last British soldiers had left Egyptian soil, Eden received the news that Nasser had nationalized the Suez Canal Company. Eden was entertaining King Faisal of Iraq, and Nuri Said, the Iraqi Prime Minister, at a state banquet at No. 10 Downing Street and Mohamed Heikal reports the scene in *Nasser: the Cairo Documents:*

31 Sir Anthony Eden, Prime Minister of Britain from 1955 to 1957.

Towards the end of the dinner a secretary came into the dining room and handed Eden a slip of paper. The Prime Minister read it and turned white with rage. He told his dinner guests that Nasser had announced the nationalization of the Suez Canal, then he lost his temper and demanded, furiously, "how can he do it . . . how can he do it . . . ?"

Nuri Said, a longstanding friend of the British in the Middle East, advised Eden:

You have only one course of action open and that is to hit, hit now and hit hard. Otherwise it will be too late . . . for if he is left alone he will finish all of us.

Much of Britain's oil from the Middle East, which was seen as essential to Britain's well-being, came through the Suez Canal. After the nationalization of the canal, Eden declared to the United States Chargé d'Affaires, Andrew Foster: "The Egyptian [Nasser] has his thumb on our windpipe [the Suez Canal]. Tell Mr Dulles [US Secretary of State] I cannot allow that". Dulles himself said that he had been told by Eden that the British "would rather risk a world war than sink to the level of a third-rate power with a depleted economy".

As soon as Eden heard of the nationalization of the Canal, he summoned an emergency cabinet meeting. The next day, 27 July, he spoke by telephone with the French Foreign Minister, Christian Pineau. The Suez Canal Company was partly owned by the French, and Eden wanted French support to use force to regain the canal and bring down Nasser and his regime. In June 1956, the French and Israelis had already concluded a secret pact against Nasser. Now Eden was proposing a Franco-British alliance against him. Pineau's view was that:

The English were incontestably humiliated by the Suez affair, coming as it did after the difficulties they had had with Egypt. They were wondering what was the best means of preventing Nasser from arriving at his ends in the Middle East . . . on many occasions during this period I heard . . . the argument that Jordan had to be held together . . . The oil factor influenced the British considerably, as it did us in Paris. (Robertson, *Crisis*)

Eden decided that action must be taken but he was anxious to get United States' support. Dulles did not want to encourage Eden to go to war, but his vague and shifting statements throughout the summer of 1956 left Eden with the sense that he would not be unsympathetic to military action by Britain against Egypt. The British and French Chiefs of Staff reported that they would not be ready to go into action against Egypt until mid September. The crisis dragged on through the summer as Britain and France tried to rouse support against Nasser and cloak their intentions with respectability. Although many nations could sympathize with their outrage, few were prepared to condone the resort to force.

Eden's cabinet was also deeply divided. Both the Leader of the House of Commons and the Minister of Defence vehemently

32 Christian Pineau, the French Foreign Minister at the time of Suez, and Golda Meir, Israel's Minister of Foreign Affairs, meeting to discuss the latest developments in the Middle East on 25 February 1958.

33 An Egyptian family group wandering through the streets of Port Said, bombed by British forces during the Suez War.

34 University students demonstrate in Manchester on 1 November 1956 against Eden's policy on Suez.

opposed the use of force. But the military machine was grinding into gear, and Eden was too far committed to abandon his goal. In late September, Pineau suggested Israeli collaboration in the Anglo-French plan, and on 3 October Pineau and Eden finally agreed to go ahead, without further discussions with Washington, in concert with an Israeli attack on Egypt at the end of October.

On 24 October Britain, France and Israel signed the secret Treaty of Sèvres. Only three copies were made, and all agreed that it should never be published.

On 29 October, Israeli forces invaded the Gaza Strip and the Sinai Peninsula and raced across towards the Canal in a highly successful lightening attack while French fighter planes and warships protected Israeli territory. In accordance with their secret Treaty, Britain and France issued an ultimatum calling upon both Israeli and Egyptian forces to ceasefire. The Israelis accepted, but Nasser naturally refused, so Britain bombed Egyptian airfields and a massive Anglo-French invasion force was despatched on 5 November, in spite of an international outcry and pressure from the United States to abandon the whole adventure.

Eden, a sick man and weakened by fever, wavered. The French were pressing him to carry out the plan, but he was appalled by the overwhelming condemnation of world opinion, in particular by the criticism from the United States and the Commonwealth. His determination faltered.

Finally, he seized at the chance offered by the United Nations to end hostilities without a total loss of face. Eden agreed to a cease-fire, much to the dismay of the French.

Britain itself was deeply divided over the Suez Crisis, which threatened to bring down Eden's Government. When Nasser sank ships to block the Canal, oil supplies were cut off, and the United States refused to help the battered British economy until Britain called off the invasion. In failing health, Eden abruptly resigned the premiership on 9 January 1957. Eden's political career was finished.

THE UPROOTED

The creation of the State of Israel in 1948 resulted in the immediate uprooting of many of the Arabs living in Palestine. Some 800,000 became homeless refugees. Many more retained their homes but were cut off from their lands and livelihood. Those who remained inside Israel found themselves strangers in their own country. They were placed under military rule, and their lands were taken for cultivation and settlement by Jews. The Palestinian Arabs, both Muslims and Christians, became a small minority in the Jewish state, and suddenly found themselves second-class citizens where before they had been on equal terms with the Jews in Palestine.

Most of the Palestinian refugees who fled took with them little more than bundles of clothes and such valuables as they could carry. More than 200,000 flooded into the Gaza Strip, overwhelming the original population of only 80,000 people. The majority fled eastwards into the mountain area occupied by Jordan's Arab Legion, which became known as the West Bank; some crossed the River Jordan to seek refuge in Jordan itself. Thousands more fled northwards to Lebanon and Syria. Some took refuge with friends and relatives, but others found shelter where they could, in caves, mosques and army barracks. Temporary tent camps were put up. These people hoped their exile would not last long, and that when the fighting stopped, they would be able to go back to their homes. But very few were able to do so.

The Zionists sent emissaries abroad to encourage Jews to immigrate to Palestine. The Israeli historian, Tom Segev, has described the Jewish migration to Israel:

Not all the immigrants to Israel came because they wanted to live there; many came because

35 A reception camp for newly arrived Jewish refugees at Shaar alliyan near Haifa, 1950.

they had no other choice. Some came because they were Zionists and believed that, being Jews, their place was in the State of Israel . . . Both in Europe and in the Arab countries there were Jews who wanted to emigrate, but not necessarily to Israel – if they could, they would have gone elsewhere.

After the establishment of the State of Israel in 1948, Jewish immigration began in earnest. Among the first to arrive were 70,000 survivors of the Nazi concentration camps and 300,000 refugees from Eastern Europe, especially Romania and Poland.

Such massive immigration put severe strains on the new state, which was not able to cope with the influx. The camps in which people were housed on arrival were grim and crowded and there was not enough food, or adequate sanitation. In March 1949, Tsvi Hermon of the Absorption Department told the Zionist Executive that conditions in the camps were unacceptable: "It is not an exaggeration to say that conditions were better in the refugee camps in Germany, after the war".

These new immigrants lacked the dedication of the early pioneers. They were not so willing to endure hardship and poverty for the sake of the Zionist ideal. Those who had been attracted by Zionist promises of a wonderful future in the promised land did not expect to face such difficulties: "People were simply cheated" stated Giora Yoseftal, a Jewish Agency Executive.

Conditions slowly improved in Israel, and more slowly also in the Palestinian refugee camps outside it. In 1950, the United Nations Relief and Works Agency for Palestine Refugees in the Near East (UNRWA) was set up to organize assistance for the thousands of Palestinian refugees. It was expected that a political solution to the conflict would be found within a few years and that UNRWA's services would then no longer be necessary, but it is still in operation today. By 1955 most of the tents in the camps run by UNRWA had been replaced by huts of some sort, and proper sanitation and water supplies were installed. The educated refugees had generally been able to find work in the Arab States, but for the mass of illiterate peasants there was no possibility of employment or resettlement. In any case, the Palestinians clung tenaciously to the dream of returning to their land and resisted any suggestion of permanent resettlement elsewhere. Although their villages had been destroyed and ploughed under by Israel and existed only in the

36 Arab refugee families queue for rice and beans provided by relief organizations.

memory of their former inhabitants, the Palestinians obstinately retained their identity. They refused to melt away and disappear into the Arab states, even though the name of their country had been erased from the map.

Where whole communities were uprooted, in Europe, in Palestine, in the Arab world, there was no possibility of going back to the old life. The old social structures were destroyed.

Fawaz Turki

Fawaz Turki was born into an Arab family in the small township of Balad al-Shaikh near Haifa, some nine years before the end of the British Mandate in Palestine.

After the departure of the British in May 1948, Fawaz and his family fled northwards to Lebanon. At first they found refuge in Sidon. In his autobiography, *The Disinherited*, he recalls the anxious beginning of their exile:

When I was a child, a few weeks after we left Palestine in 1948, I used to . . . listen to the radio at precisely three o'clock every day. The voice from Radio Israel (or Radio Tel Aviv, or whatever damn name it had) used to come on to announce the Messages. Silence would fill the space around us. Tension would grip even the children. "From Abu Shareef, and Jameela, Samir and Kamal in Haifa," the words would come across the air. "To our Leila and her husband Fouad. Are you in Lebanon? We are all well". . . . The dispassionate voice continues: "From Ibrahim Shawki to his wife Zamzam. I have moved to Jaffa. Your father is safe with us".

For a whole hour, families would listen

37 The next generation of Palestinian freedom fighters rehearse their roles with wooden weapons in a refugee camp near Beirut.

38 Palestinians attending a school at a refugee camp.

anxiously to hear from relatives left behind in Israel and separated from the rest of the family.

After a few months in Sidon, we moved again, a Palestinian family of six heading to a refugee camp in Beirut, impotent with hunger, frustration, and incomprehension. But there we encountered other families equally helpless, equally baffled, who like us never had enough to eat, never enough to offer books and education to their children, never enough to face an imminent winter.

Fawaz spent his time doing odd jobs to earn money, hanging about with other youngsters and stealing. Then he got the chance to go to a school run by an evangelical organization that offered a free education to the children of Palestinian refugees. Eventually he left the Evangelists, and enrolled in a high school run by a Palestinian organization with a scholarship from UNRWA.

He soon became active in student politics, and joined the Syrian Social Nationalist Party. Fawaz became extremely suspicious of Nasser because he believed that Nasser was only interested in Arab nationalism in order to assert Egypt's leadership over the Arab world. Yet many Palestinians believed that Nasser wanted to liberate their homeland.

At home there were tense scenes when I would argue mercilessly with my poor father, ridiculing his naïve grasp of Middle Eastern politics, or in desperation, rip Nasser's picture off the wall and spit on it. . . . In those days of emotional crisis, in those last years of his on earth, he had nothing except hope. And he hoped. And a million people hoped. And I relentlessly attacked him, robbing him of that system of logic he had constructed around himself to interpret the tragedy that had befallen him and his people.

Fawaz joined demonstrations and even got arrested by the Lebanese police on one occasion but was allowed to go after a couple of days in gaol. Then in 1957, he graduated from high school and was awarded a scholarship to study in England, where he spent three-and-a-half years.

I returned to the Middle East more embittered, more disillusioned, more unhappy than when I left. There was a rage within me. An anger. A hate. A fury that was almost animal in its intensity. I had been cheated by the world, by the gods, and by history . . . I hated being dispossessed of a nation and an identity . . . I hated being a hybrid, an outcast, and a zero.

He travelled to Damascus to visit his uncle. Travelling reinforced his sense of isolation as an outcast, different from other people who have a nationality and rights:

In Beirut, I had to register my return to Lebanon

with the police. I had also reported to the Damascus police upon arrival and departure, producing two photographs each time. When it comes to travel, the lot of a refugee is not a pleasant one.

At 22, restless and angry, he decided to travel to India and Nepal, where he lived in spiritual communities and found a certain peace of mind. He stayed there about three years. Like other young, articulate and educated Palestinians, he had felt estranged and helpless. Their parents were resigned and defeated, but they, the forgotten generation, were angry:

The Palestinians were the people from whom everything was taken and nothing was heard. They were the people on whose behalf all the threats against the enemy were made, and on whose behalf war was to be waged . . . Like puppets on a string, the Palestinians and their cause were constantly used whenever masters of ceremony took to the stage to amuse the masses, to hear themselves speak, to gain prestige.

On 5 June 1967, war broke out. The Israelis inflicted a devastating defeat on the Arab states and left Arab society reeling from the shock. The Palestinians started to take matters into their own hands. They were not content to be referred to, as in UN Resolution 242, as nothing more than a "refugee problem". The Palestinian political and guerrilla movements grew and forced their grievances on the world's attention by hijacking aircraft and other spectacular actions. Fawaz returned from his retreat in the East, and regained his sense of identity. At last he was no longer alone, shamefaced and in hiding. He was proud to shout to the world that he was a Palestinian.

39 Yasser Arafat, the leader of the Palestine Liberation Organization.

Yuval Aloni

Yuval Aloni was born into a Jewish family in North Yemen, at a time when the Yemen was very isolated and poor. He lived in a village that consisted only of Jews and was a day's walk from Ta'izz, one of the most important towns.

Until an army revolt in 1963 heralded the revolution, Yemeni society was still the same

40 Yemeni Jews being transported by plane to Israel as part of "Operation Magic Carpet".

as in medieval times. The country was governed by an autocratic and all-powerful ruler, the Imam. Muslims were the first-class citizens in the state, and Christians and Jews had only secondary status. There was no modern education system or any modern influence at all.

The Jewish community of Yemen was religious, and the boys all studied the Torah and the works of the sages. Yuval enjoyed studying:

My ambition was to be the Clever Pupil, the very best pupil. . . . When I say we studied only religion, it was the same for the Arabs – they learned about their religion and we learned about ours. But we were less than they were, and ironically that is how we became rich . . . As inferiors, we were not entitled to pay tax. But the Arab was a privileged citizen and he had to pay tax.

I never felt inferior. Look how it goes: everywhere I went I had to be lower than an Arab in height. A Jew on a donkey could not pass an Arab on foot. God forbid that you were higher than he! We were not allowed to own a horse or wear a turban or carry a weapon, because these were symbols of nobility. We were not allowed to have any of the things that belonged to people who were proud and free. But being Jewish, in my eyes, makes me a thousand times, an infinity of times, higher. I'm the chosen one. (McNeish, *Belonging*)

The Yemeni Jewish community believed that they were condemned to live in exile because of a local tradition. It was believed that in ancient times when the King of Persia freed the Jews in Babylon and the Prophet Ezra called on Jews everywhere to come back and rebuild Jerusalem, the Jews of Yemen had refused to return. They had said that to return to Jerusalem then would be anticipating the coming of the Messiah. So Ezra had cursed them to remain in exile in Yemen in suffering and without peace. Yuval was told when he was born that he was in exile, as his father and grandfather had been before him. All the time the community was waiting for the day of redemption.

I was in school when the day came. Nobody walked into the village and said, "Hola! the State of Israel is declared". None of us sat down and took a count and said, "Will we go? Won't we?" It wasn't like that. It was in the air. The news was immediate, instantaneous. For us, it was the Messiah.

After travelling by camel to Ta'izz, and by truck to the British colony of Aden, they waited weeks in Aden for the planes to take them to Israel. They brought nothing with them except the holy books, the Torah scrolls. They refused to take anything of value, except money needed for expenses on the way. They were not going to take impure things that would defile the holy country. Finally the Dakota aeroplanes brought them to Israel.

When we arrived we were taken to a transit camp and we couldn't believe our senses. I had never seen such a thing before: a Jew with a spade in his hand. They were working in a citrus grove, digging holes. Have you seen those immense holes they have to pump water? In Yemen we had slaves doing these things, not citizens...

We were taken to a settlement in Galilee and my father had to clean the site of stones, break rocks with a hoe. He collapsed. Yet he would not complain against the land. He found that everything was so different from the scriptures, yet he felt it was forbidden to voice complaints against the land – he accepted everything, and my father and I were in terrible conflict. I swung from one extreme to the other. My state of shock lasted six months, then when I awoke, I cut off my earlocks and threw away my "kipah" [skullcap]. I lost my religion completely. Now I have come to a position of balance... Even if I

41 Jews planting orange trees. Many were planted over abandoned Palestinian Arab villages in the 1950s.

have lost my religion I have lost nothing of my country. Can you understand? My soul can never leave this place. I would never think of emigrating, never... I care very much that my

42 Yemeni Jews in Israel making baskets. European Jews looked down on Jews from Arab lands as primitive and backward.

people should be continued. I was a second-class citizen. It is a thing you cannot forget. Here the land is ours and it does not matter if it is good – it is like a man and his son – if the son is not so good, so what. Will he kill him?

The difficulties facing the Jews from the Arab states and Asia (Oriental Jews) did not stop at culture shock. The Zionist establishment that ruled Israel in the early days was European in origin, outlook and mentality. They regarded the Oriental Jews as little better than the Arabs. They looked down upon them as primitive and backward and hoped that they would soon become Westernized simply by coming to live in an Israel that promoted a Western cultural style. The rich cultural heritage that the Oriental Jews brought with them was neglected and despised.

Ezra Ben-Hakkam Eliyahu, in an article about the Sephardic (or Oriental) Jews published in 1978, wrote:

In 1962 a North African Zionist leader observed that there were more North African Jewish professors at the Sorbonne [Paris University] than North African Jewish students at the Hebrew University of Jerusalem. . . Sephardim are often accused of lacking a "pioneering spirit". The truth is that hundreds of moshavim [co-operative farms] were set up by them, but the Zionist establishment did not provide them with the finance, equipment and land in the same way that they had the Ashkenazi [European Jewish] settlements. (Middle East International March 1978.)

Immigrants from Eastern Europe who arrived in the 1960s were instantly offered newly-built flats in nice suburbs. The Oriental Jews, in contrast, were living in poor accommodation in over-crowded slums or in the shabby neglected development towns to which they had been forcibly directed in the early years.

Yuval Aloni served in Israel's wars with its Arab neighbours and later enrolled in a branch of an American University. He summed up his experiences in these words:

You come from a feudal society, like it was in Europe in the twelfth century. You go through a lot, something like two hundred and eighty generations in a lifetime – it's not simple! I feel like somebody who has lived for seven hundred years.

Erika Lewin (1911-   )

Erika Lewin was born in Czernowitz, part of the Austro-Hungarian Empire in what is now Romania. In 1940, she and her family were arrested by Russian troops and taken east, where they were forced to stay even after the war. Although many of the survivors of the Nazi concentration camps did go to Israel in the years after the war, Stalin's regime in the Soviet Union made it impossible for Erika or her family to leave.

In 1955, Erika began to apply to go to Israel as she had read once in a newspaper that Austrian citizens could be repatriated. The Austrian consul in Moscow was sympathetic, but thought it might be difficult since they were in the depths of Siberia. She recalls in *Belonging*:

This other woman applied to return to her home in Bessarabia, but we never wanted to return. There was no one there anymore. So I applied for Israel. They turned down the first application.

And then the second. The third, and the fourth. The relatives had to beg, in Russian, to explain that the entire family had been wiped out by the Nazis, that there were just the two of us, two women, alone and old . . . that they should allow us to join our family. And then, in 1963, they gave us permission.

Erika and her mother had to renounce their rights to Soviet citizenship, and after going through all the elaborate processes required by the Soviet bureaucracy, they arrived in Vienna on their way to Israel. Erika sent a postcard to her distant relations in Israel but did not expect that anyone would know they were coming.

But the welcome! We arrived in Haifa on December 15, 1963. They were so loving, even strangers shared everything with us . . . The presents, and a flat – right away, on the first day. I felt like a queen. They said, "You can live anywhere you like, Tel Aviv, Haifa, Kiriat Tivon. . ." But we wanted to be in Jerusalem.

Erika was lucky. The hardships of the early years were past, and new immigrants from the Soviet Union were especially welcomed by the Israeli establishment. For a long time Erika could not get over the fact that the pious American Jews who lived next door to them in Jerusalem could walk freely down the street every Saturday with their prayer shawls without any fear of hostility. It was quite safe to look Jewish.

43 Hitler, the German leader responsible for the horrifying Nazi policy of exterminating Jews in Europe.

44 Jewish survivors from the Nazi Holocaust in Europe arriving in Haifa, Israel.

Raymonda Hawa Tawil

Raymonda Hawa Tawil was born in 1940 into a Greek Orthodox Christian Arab family living in Acre in Palestine.

In her book *My home, my prison* in which she tells the story of her life, Raymonda recounts the effect of the disorder in Palestine as the British prepared to leave in 1948. At that time she was staying with her aunt in Haifa (because her mother had been divorced):

In the eighth year of my life, I witnessed terrifying things: men with guns and helmets – a man killed outside our home – houses blown up. My aunt was too weak, physically and psychologically, to deal with the situation. She had her own five boys to take care of, as well as me, and she sank into a terrified passivity, unable to do more than wonder out loud: "Who will bury the dead?"

She returned to the comparative safety of a convent school in Nazareth but was concerned about her family after the war in 1948:

There was still no news of Father or of the other members of my family. One day a nun told me that there was no one to pay my fees. "We have to consider you as an orphan", she said bluntly. From her point of view, it was a simple administrative matter; with no one paying for me, I was considered a charity case, and therefore they had to transfer me to the orphans' wing.

One day, some time later, her mother turned up to visit her at the convent. Raymonda was overjoyed. A short time later, her father also reappeared.

I burst into tears of joy on seeing him again, after all these months of uncertainty whether he was alive or dead. I told him of my transfer to the orphans' section; later, when he went to pay my tuition fees, he asked pointedly who had spread the news of his death? The nuns were too embarrassed to reply, but later they scolded me for telling him!

But the borders created by the war had divided the family. Her two brothers attended a boarding school in East Jerusalem which was now in Jordan.

In 1952, Raymonda was moved to a different convent school in Haifa, where all the other girls were Jewish. In Nazareth, all the girls had been from Arab families, Muslim and Christian. The Jewish girls were mostly from Europe where they had been baptized to save them from the Nazis. Many of these families had retained their Christian ties and sent them to the convent schools, but the Israeli government wanted them to attend government Jewish schools, and later the numbers of Jewish girls in convent schools declined sharply.

Raymonda became friendly with some of these girls.

One of my school friends was a Jewish girl named Dvora; she was very sweet, and I loved her. One day, she invited me home, and I went along. When we neared her house, I suddenly realized where she was taking me. Her family now occupied my aunt's house! . . . I bore no resentment against Dvora or her parents. I sensed that they, too, felt the injustice of occupying someone else's home. "Soon, the Arab refugees will be allowed to return to their homes", they reassured me, "and our government will build new houses for us. . . and then Jews and Arabs will live together in peace". They were as naive as I; neither they nor I knew the true intentions of their government. My aunt was never permitted to return, and Dvora's family remained in that house for twenty-five years.

Some time later the Israeli authorities dismissed her mother from her job as a social worker for "security reasons". She had,

45 The Mandelbaum Gate in Jerusalem.

indeed, been "in correspondence with an enemy country"; she had received a letter from one of her sons in Jordan, with a snapshot of himself, via a relative who had forwarded it from Europe. This letter branded her as a "security risk" and she lost her job. Unable to find anything else, she went to work as a seamstress at a home for delinquent Arab children. Raymonda developed a fierce hostility towards the state that discriminated against her people, although she was impressed by many of the individual Israelis (mostly left-wingers) who stood up for the rights of the Palestinian minority. Her parents disagreed fundamentally over the sort of future she should pursue.

Mother wanted me to remain with her; I was her only remaining child. She was ambitious for me. She wanted me to study and make a career for myself, to become emancipated and independent. Father's view was quite different . . . Sharing the aristocratic, traditionalist view of his class, he looked down on the Arabs who remained in Israel: they were inferior beings, uncultured peasants with whom he had little in common . . . He spoke in glowing terms of the broader horizons of Arab society in other lands, especially Lebanon. He urged me to leave Israel and make my home elsewhere.

Mother held the opposite view. She knew Arab society only too well; she knew what kind of life awaited me as a woman in an Arab country.

Raymonda was torn but in the end chose to leave, wanting to get to know her brothers whom she had seen only once a year at Christmas for a few hours. In March 1957, at the age of 17, she crossed into Jordan through the Mandelbaum Gate in Jerusalem, leaving Israel forever. She had had to renounce her Israeli nationality, so once she left she would not be permitted to return.

She experienced something of a culture shock when she went to live with her brother in Amman. Arab society was very conservative and traditional, and she rebelled against the restrictions placed on her freedom of movement.

I found myself in a strange dilemma. In Israel, I would belong to a despised minority and be treated as a second-class citizen. All the same, as a woman, my personal lot would be much better than in Jordan. A difficult choice: humiliation as an Arab or repression as a woman – which is better?

She regretted her decision and asked to return to Israel, but the Jordanian government would no more allow her to go back to "enemy territory" than the Israelis would permit her return. She had to stay, and make the best of it. Unwilling to remain indefinitely a burden on her relatives, she agreed to marry Da'ud Tawil, a prosperous bank manager from a well-known Jaffa family. He was much older than her, but sociable and likable.

She started a new, uneventful life as a married, middle-class woman at first in Irbid, on the East Bank of the Jordan, and later in Nablus, on the West Bank. She had three children in the first four years of marriage. In 1961, just after the birth of her third child, her mother was allowed for a one-day visit through the Mandelbaum Gate. Although thrilled to see her grandchildren, her mother was horrified at her conformity with the old traditions and restricted existence. "I gave you independence!" she reminded me reproachfully."

It was the last time she saw her mother. The next year she did not arrive at the Mandelbaum Gate. She was dead, and Raymonda felt guilty that she had died disappointed in her only daughter. She started to organize cultural activities with a group of like-minded women, but soon discovered that Palestinian nationalist activities incurred as much suspicion and repression from the Jordanian authorities as they did from the Israelis. She became a member of the Arab Women's Union and worked as a journalist. Her activities were not at all to the liking of

46 An Arab refugee woman, carrying her possessions on her way to the Allenby Bridge leading to Jordan, June 1967.

47 The convent of the Terra Santa in Nazareth.

either her husband or traditional and conservative circles in Nablus, where her contacts with Western diplomats were regarded with suspicion and it was thought improper for a woman to "push herself forward".

In June 1967, the Israelis occupied Nablus and the rest of the Jordanian-held West Bank.

The morning after the occupation, we awake to find our house an island in a human sea. Astonished, I gaze out of the window at one of the most amazing, horrifying scenes I have ever beheld. Outside our house, in the road, in the olive groves, there are literally thousands of people – old, young, families with children, pregnant women, cripples. In their arms or on their backs they carry bundles with a few possessions. Young women clutch babies. Everywhere, the same exhausted, broken figures, the stunned, desperate faces...

My mind goes back to 1948, and the mass exodus of Palestinians. My God, I think, is this going to happen again?

Raymonda once more flung herself into political activity, taking advantage of her knowledge of Hebrew and Israeli society. Although accused of collaboration for contacts with sympathetic Israelis, she became well-known abroad as a committed nationalist who championed the right of the Palestinians to establish their own state alongside Israel in historic Palestine.

GLOSSARY

Anti-Semitism Hatred of Jews on racial and religious grounds.

Arab League (also known as League of Arab States) Founded in March 1945; designed to strengthen ties between Arab states and to co-ordinate their policies and activities.

Arab Legion A small but efficient armed force built up by the British during the early 1920s in Transjordan. It played a significant role in the fighting with Israel during 1948.

Arab Women's Union Founded in 1921 by Hajja Andalib Al-Amad of Nablus, the Union did important welfare work for women, combating illiteracy and organizing vocational training for girls. It also organized political demonstrations against the British and later against Jordanian rule over the West Bank.

Ashkenazi (Jews) Jews from the communities of Eastern Europe. The terms Ashkenazim and Sephardim are derived from interpretations given by mediaeval rabbis to the names of peoples which appear in Genesis x of the Bible.

Baghdad Pact Originally an agreement between Iraq and Turkey for co-operation and defence signed on 24 February 1955. Britain joined on 5 April, Pakistan on 23 September and Iran on 3 November 1955. The United States never joined, although it participated in several of the Pact's most influential committees, especially those dealing with military matters and security.

Balfour Declaration A statement by British Foreign Secretary, Arthur J. Balfour, on 2 November 1917 in a letter to Lord Rothschild of the Zionist Organization promising British Government support for the establishment of a national home in Palestine for the Jewish people.

Betar A para-military right-wing Zionist youth group founded during the 1920s by Vladimir Jabotinsky.

Eretz Israel The (biblical) Land of Israel.

Gaza Strip A narrow coastal strip in south-west Palestine occupied and held by the Egyptian army in 1948. Many Arab refugees from those parts of Palestine occupied by Israel took refuge there. It remained in Arab hands until June 1967 when it was occupied by Israeli forces during the Six-Day War.

Golan Heights Upland region on Syria's border with Israel. Strategically important because it overlooks Jewish settlements in the plain below. Captured by the Israeli army in June 1967; annexed to Israel in December 1981.

Greater Syria After the division of the Syrian Province of the Ottoman Empire into several small political units after the First World War Palestine, Lebanon, Jordan and Syria – many people looked for their re-unification into one large state, often referred to as Greater Syria.

Haganah Jewish militia formed to protect Jewish settlements in Palestine; it developed into the Israeli army.

Hijaz The western coastal strip of modern Saudi Arabia that includes the Muslim holy cities of Mecca and Medina. Until the end of the First World War Hijaz formed a part of the Ottoman Empire.

Irgun The Irgun Zvai Leumi (National Military Organization) was a right-wing Zionist terrorist group responsible for attacks on Arab civilians and British personnel and institutions.

Jewish Agency Britain's mandate for Palestine provided for the establishment of a Jewish Agency to co-operate with the British administration of Palestine in matters affecting the establishment of the Jewish National Home. Established in 1929 its basic aims were to facilitate Jewish immigration to Palestine, to advance Hebrew language and culture, to purchase land in Palestine for Jews, and to develop agriculture and settlements for Jewish immigrants.

Kibbutz Jewish communal village where all property is owned in common by the members.

Knesset The Israeli Parliament.

Mandate Power conferred on a state by the League of Nations in 1919 to govern a different region. The Mandatory Power was supposed to prepare the region under its rule for eventual independence.

Mapai Land of Israel Workers' Party, founded in 1929 and led by Ben-Gurion, generally known as the Labour Party.

Moshav Co-operative village where each family has its own plot of land, but marketing and other activities are handled co-operatively.

Mufti [of Jerusalem] An official Muslim expert

in Islamic law who was also a dignitary of some standing in major cities of the Ottoman Empire.

Nazi Holocaust The horrifying Nazi policy of exterminating Jews in Europe which reached frightening proportions after the outbreak of the Second World War. Nazi Germany's racist policy killed 6 million Jews in Nazi-occupied Europe and left thousands of Jewish refugees who had been forced to flee their homes.

Rabbi Religious leader of a Jewish congregation. The Orthodox Rabbis adhere to a very strict and traditional interpretation of Jewish religious law.

Sephardi (Jews) Jews from Mediterranean countries (see also Ashkenazi). The term is often used to include all Jews not from Western backgrounds.

Shaikhdoms Small Arab Gulf states ruled by a shaikh or tribal leader.

Sharif [of Mecca] A title used to signify a descendant of the Prophet Mohamed. It was also a title given to the guardian of the Holy Cities of Mecca and Medina under the Ottoman Empire.

Sinai Peninsula Triangular-shaped desert area that forms the landbridge between Asia and Africa, bordered in the west by the Suez Canal and the Gulf of Suez, in the east by the Gulf of Aqaba.

Stern Gang An extreme right-wing Zionist terrorist group which split away from the Irgun.

Tiran, Straits of The Straits of Tiran at the southernmost tip of the Sinai Peninsula control access to Eilat, Israel's only non-Mediterranean port.

Torah Scrolls Torah is a Hebrew word meaning "teaching" (but often translated as "law" and refers to the written scriptures of Judaism – the five books of Mosaic Law (incorporated into the Old Testament of the Christian Bible). In Synagogues, a copy of the Torah written on a Scroll in traditional style is used for the readings.

UNEF (United Nations Emergency Force) Established in 1956-7 by the UN General Assembly to supervise the ceasefire following the joint attack on Egypt by Israel, Britain and France in 1956. Egypt agreed to the stationing of the UNEF in Egypt and the Egyptian-occupied Gaza Strip. Israel refused to have it on its territory.

United Arab Republic In 1958 Syria and Egypt merged into one state with Nasser as President. Syria withdrew from the union in 1961.

United Nations (UN) Founded on 24 October 1945, the organization aims to maintain international peace and security and to develop international co-operation in economic, social, cultural and humanitarian problems. Since its establishment the UN has dealt continuously with many Middle Eastern problems. The one most persistently on its agenda has been the Palestine question.

UNRWA United Nations Relief and Works Agency for Palestine Refugees in the Near East, created by a UN Resolution in 1949, and established in 1950 to care for Palestinians who became refugees as a result of the creation of Israel in 1948.

West Bank Name given to the mountainous region of Palestine lying to the west of the River Jordan. Occupied by the Arab Legion in 1948 and annexed by King Abdullah of Jordan to his kingdom. Occupied by Israeli forces during the Six-Day War of June 1967.

Yiddish Language spoken by Jewish communities in Eastern Europe, a compound of corrupted Hebrew and old German.

Yishuv Jewish community in Palestine before the establishment of the State of Israel

Zionism Movement of Jewish national revival founded in the late nineteenth century for the return of the Jewish people to Palestine. The name is derived from "Zion", one of the biblical names for Jerusalem.

Date List

1914	First World War breaks out.
1915	Britain agrees to recognize an independent Arab state.
1916	Sharif Husain declares the Arab Revolt against Ottoman rule.
1917	In the Balfour Declaration, Britain agrees to support the establishment of a Jewish National Home in Palestine.
1918	Germany and Turkey are defeated and the First World War comes to an end.
1919	The victorious Allies hold a peace conference at Versailles.
1920	Syria declares itself independent and Faisal is crowned king. The French occupy Damascus and drive him out. The League of Nations awards Mandate over Syria and Lebanon to France and Iraq and Palestine to Britain.
1923	Britain's Mandate over Palestine is confirmed.
1933	Hitler comes to power in Germany and Nazi influence grows.
1936-8	Arab Revolt in Palestine against British rule.
1939	British White Paper on Palestine proposes to limit further Jewish immigration. Second World War breaks out.
1942	Extraordinary Zionist Conference held at Biltmore Hotel in New York.
1945	Nazi Germany is defeated. Second World War ends.
1946	King David Hotel in Jerusalem blown up by Zionists.
1947	Britain hands back its Mandate over Palestine to UN. UN votes in favour of partition.
1948	Zionists attack Arab areas in Palestine. Britain leaves and State of Israel is declared. First Arab-Israeli war. 800,000 Palestinians become refugees.
1949	Negotiations at Rhodes lead to Armistices between Israel and the Arab states.
1951	King Abdullah of Jordan is assassinated in Jerusalem.
1954	Nasser becomes President of Egypt.
1955	Nasser opposes the Baghdad Pact and concludes a major arms deal with Czechoslovakia.
1956	Nasser nationalizes the Suez Canal leading to the Suez Crisis. Britain, France and Israel invade Egypt.
1958	Syria and Egypt unite to form the United Arab Republic (UAR).
1961	Syria secedes from the UAR.
1966	A new government comes to power in Syria and encourages Palestinian guerrilla attacks on Israel.
1967	Rising tensions lead to the Six-Day War in June in which Israel conquers the remainder of historic Palestine, and Syrian and Egyptian territory.

BOOKS FOR FURTHER READING

General
H. Bleaney and R. Lawless, *The First Day of the Six Day War*, Batsford, 1990
H. Bleaney and R. Lawless, *The Post-War World: the Middle East since 1945*, Batsford, 1989
D. Hirst, *The gun and the olive branch*, Faber, 1977; rev. ed. 1983
W. Laqueur and B. Rubin, *The Israel-Arab reader: a documentary history of the Middle East conflict*, 4th edition, Facts on File, 1985
M. Robinson, *Israel and the Arabs*, 2nd edition, Penguin, 1982

The Zionists
K. Bain, *The March to Zion*, Texas University Press, 1979
Bar-Zohar, M. *Ben-Gurion*, Weidenfeld and Nicholson, 1979
Moshe Dayan, *Story of my Life*, Weidenfeld and Nicolson, 1976
L. Brenner, *The Iron Wall: Zionist revisionism from Jabotinstin to Shamir*, Zed Books, 1984
S. Teveth, *Ben-Gurion and the Palestinian Arabs: from peace to war*, Oxford University Press, 1985

The Arabs
G. Furlonge, *Palestine is my country. The story of Musa Alami*, Murray, 1969
R. Stephens, *Nasser*, Penguin, 1971
M.C. Wilson, *King Abdullah, Britain and the making of Jordan*, Cambridge University Press, 1977

The Outsiders
Folke Bernadotte, *To Jerusalem*, Hodder and Stoughton, 1951
A. Ilan, *Bernadotte in Palestine, 1948*, Macmillan, 1989
W.R. Louis, *The British Empire and the Middle East 1945-51*, Oxford University Press, 1984
A. Nutting, *No end of a lesson: the story of Suez*, Constable, 1967
T. Robertson, *Crisis: the inside story of the Suez conspiracy*, Hutchinson, 1964

The Uprooted
I. Bendt & J. Downing, *We shall return: women of Palestine*, Zed Books, 1982
J. McNeish, *Belonging. Conversations with men and women who have chosen to make Israel their home*, Collins, 1980
T. Segev, *1949: the first Israelis*, The Free Press, New York, 1986
R.H. Tawil, *My Home, My Prison*, Zed Books, 1983
Fawaz Turki, *The disinherited: journal of a Palestinian exile*, Monthly Review Press, 1972

INDEX

Abdul Hamid II, Sultan of Turkey 9, 27
Abdullah, King of Jordan 6, 27-31
Alami, Musa 24-27
Aloni, Yuval 51-54
Altalena (ship) 17
Amman 29, 58
Arab Development Society 25, 27
Arab League 25, 28, 40
Arab Legion 5, 28-31, 47
Arab nationalism 3, 6, 24, 33, 50
Arab revolt in Palestine 1936-38 3, 4, 11, 18
Arab States 5, 6, 8, 12, 15, 18, 23, 48, 49
Aswan High Dam 32
Attlee, Clement 37

Baghdad Pact 26, 32
Balfour, Arthur 3
Balfour Declaration 3, 10, 36
Begin, Menachem 14-18
Beirut 25, 26, 50
Ben-Gurion, David 10-13, 14, 17, 18, 20 36
Bernadotte, Folke 17, 18, 29, 37, 39-43
Betar movement 14
Bevin, Ernest 4
Boys' Camp 27
Britain 3, 4, 6, 7, 10, 13, 14, 18, 23, 24, 25, 27-33, 36, 37, 40, 41, 44, 46, 49, 56

Cairo 8, 12, 31, 33, 35
Churchill, Winston 4, 27, 37, 43
Czechoslovakia 7, 12, 32

Damascus 24, 25, 50, 51
Dayan, Moshe 13, 18-22
Deir Yassin 14, 15

Eden, Anthony 43-46
Egypt 5, 6, 12, 13, 18, 21-23, 31-35, 38, 40, 43, 44, 46, 50
Eisenhower, President 7
Eretz Israel 18
Eshkol, Levi 20, 21

Faisal, King of Iraq 43
Farouk, King of Egypt 6, 31
First World War 3, 10, 23, 24, 27, 36, 43
France 3, 6, 7, 13, 17, 23, 27, 33, 44, 46

Gaza 6, 7, 18, 20, 22, 46, 47
Germany 3, 4, 10, 11, 18, 39
Glubb Pasha 5, 30
Golan Heights 8

Haganah 4, 11, 12, 14, 15, 17, 18
Haifa 14, 49, 55, 56
Herzl, Theodor 9
Hijaz 27

Hitler, Adolf 10
Holocaust 10
Husain, King of Jordan 6, 26, 31
Husain, Sharif of Mecca 27

Iraq 3, 23, 27, 33, 40
Irgun Zvai Leumi 4, 11, 14, 15, 17

Jaffa 15
Jerusalem 4, 6, 10, 14, 18, 20, 21, 22, 24, 25, 29, 30, 31, 41, 43, 55, 56
Jewish Agency 4, 10, 11, 14, 48
Jewish immigration 3, 10, 12, 36, 37, 41, 47, 48, 54, 55
Jewish Legion 10
Jewish National Home 3, 10, 23, 36
Jordan 5, 6, 8, 14, 18, 22, 23, 25-28, 30, 31, 34, 40, 47, 56-59
Jordan River 18, 34, 47
Jordan Valley 18, 25, 27

King David Hotel 14

Labour party (of Israel) 10, 14, 18, 20
Lebanon 3, 6, 12, 18, 23, 34, 40, 47, 49 50, 57
Lewin, Erika 54-55
Lydda 18, 30

Mandate, British 3, 4, 10, 11, 12, 14, 17, 18, 24, 36, 49
Mandelbaum Gate 57, 58
Mapai Party, *see* Labour Party (of Israel)
Meir, Golda 22, 45 (picture)
Mufti of Jerusalem 6

Nasser, Gamal Abdul 6-8, 13, 18, 31-35, 43, 44, 50
Nationalization of the Suez Canal Company 7, 13, 43, 44
Nazareth 56
Nazis 3, 10, 11, 14, 37, 39, 40, 48, 54, 55

Occupied Territories 8, 22
Ottoman Empire 3, 9, 10, 23, 24, 27, 36

Palestine 3-6, 8-12, 14, 17, 18, 23-31, 36, 37, 39-42, 47, 49, 56, 59
Palestinian guerrillas 8, 20, 34, 51
Partition Plan 1947 4-6, 14, 18, 23, 28, 37, 38
Pineau, Christian 44, 46
Port Said 7, 12

Rabin, Yitzhak 21
Ramleh 18, 30
Refugees 6, 8, 22, 25, 30, 36, 37, 40-43, 47, 48, 50, 51, 56

Rhodes 6, 18, 40
Rothschild, Lord 3

Said, Nuri 43, 44
Second World War 4, 9, 10, 11, 23, 36, 43
Sharett, Moshe 13, 41, 42
Sharon, Ariel 18
Sinai Peninsula 5, 7, 8, 13, 18, 20, 33, 35, 46
Six-Day War 1967 8, 13, 22, 35, 51, 59
Stalin, Joseph 54
Stern Gang 4, 11, 14, 43
Suez Canal 7, 13, 31, 32, 33, 35, 43, 44
Suez War 1956 7, 13, 18, 20, 33, 44-46
Syria 3, 6, 8, 12, 18, 23, 27, 28, 33, 34, 35, 40, 47

Tawil, Raymonda Hawa 56-59
Tel Aviv 5, 17, 20, 40, 55
Tiran, Straits of 8
Transjordan (*see* also Jordan) 3, 12, 27, 29, 41, 43
Truman, Harry 36-39
Turki, Fawaz 49-51
Turks, *see* Ottoman Empire

UN Partition Plan, *see* Partition Plan 1947
UNEF, *see* United Nations Emergency Force
Union of Soviet Socialist Republics (USSR) 8, 14, 28, 32, 35, 36, 54
United Nations (UN) 4, 6, 7, 12, 14, 17, 18, 23, 26, 29, 33, 36-41, 43, 51
United Nations Emergency Force (UNEF) 7, 8
United Nations Relief and Works Agency for Palestine Refugees in the Near East (UNRWA) 26, 48, 50
United States of America (USA) 7, 10, 13, 22, 28, 29, 30, 32, 33, 36-39, 44, 46
UNRWA, *see* United Nations Relief and Works Agency
USA, *see* United States of America
USSR, *see* Union of Soviet Socialist Republics

Weizmann, Chaim 7 (picture), 38
West Bank 6, 8, 22, 26, 30, 31, 47, 58, 59
White Paper 1939 3, 11
World Zionist Organization 14, 38

Yemen 51, 52
Yishuv 10

Zionism 9, 10, 22
Zionists 3, 4, 9, 10-12, 14, 17, 18, 23, 24, 36, 37, 40, 47, 48